WINDOWS ON OUR WORLD

THE HOUGHTON MIFFLIN SOCIAL STUDIES PROGRAM

ME
THINGS WE DO
THE WORLD AROUND US
WHO ARE WE?
PLANET EARTH
THE UNITED STATES
THE WAY PEOPLE LIVE

WINDOWS ON OUR WORLD

WHO ARE WE?

SARA S. BEATTIE

DOLORES GRECO

General Editor   LEE F. ANDERSON

HOUGHTON MIFFLIN COMPANY   BOSTON

Atlanta   Dallas   Geneva, Illinois   Hopewell, New Jersey   Palo Alto   Toronto

ABOUT THE AUTHORS

Sara S. Beattie is an elementary teacher and Cross-Cultural Specialist in the Brookline, Massachusetts, school system. Co-author of a number of textbooks, she has been a playwright for Boston educational television and is the author of several books for children.

Dolores Greco is a lecturer in social studies methods and child development, and a supervisor of student teachers at Queens College of the City University of New York. She is a former elementary school teacher and counselor and was a recent consultant to the New York City Center for Urban Education.

SOURCES AND ACKNOWLEDGMENTS

Page 40: Poem "In the Evening Glow," from *I See the Wind.* Copyright © by Kazue Mizumara. Reprinted by permission of Thomas Y. Crowell Company, Inc.; "At the edge of the World," from *Singing for Power, The Song Magic of the Papago Indians of Southern Arizona* by Ruth Underhill. Originally published by the University of California Press; reprinted by permission of The Regents of the University of California. Page 71: "Which Is Better, the Sun or the Moon?" adapted from *The Man in the Moon: Sky Tales from Many Lands* by Alta Jablow and Carl Withers. Copyright © 1969 by Alta Jablow and Carl Withers. Reprinted by permission of Holt, Rinehart and Winston, Inc. Pages 168–173: Adapted with permission from "The Battle of Allatoona," by Eugene H. Methvin, *The Reader's Digest,* May, 1973. Copyright 1973 by The Reader's Digest Assn., Inc.

Printed in the United States of America
Library of Congress Catalog Card Number: 74–18541
ISBN: 0–395–20133–0

GENERAL EDITOR

Lee F. Anderson is Professor of Education and Political Science at Northwestern University and co-director of the Political Science Education Project for the American Political Science Association. His numerous published articles and papers include the frequently reprinted "Global Education: Long Range Goals and Objectives." He is a member of the Social Science Education Consortium and the National Council for Social Studies.

SKILLS CONSULTANT

Barbara J. Winston is Assistant Professor of Geography and Environmental Studies at Northeastern Illinois University and is engaged in the university's teacher education program. Previously she taught in the Palatine and Park Ridge, Illinois, public school systems. She developed the "Building Map Skills" section in this textbook.

VALUES CONSULTANT

Charlotte C. Anderson, a specialist in values education in elementary schools, is presently completing doctoral studies in Elementary Social Studies Education at Northwestern University. She has been teaching at Northeastern Illinois University, and is a member of the National Council for the Social Studies Committee on Social Justice for Women.

READING CONSULTANT

Roger E. Johnson is Associate Professor of Education at the University of South Florida. He is an elementary social studies consultant for Florida public schools and a reading adviser to a number of local school systems.

EVALUATION CONSULTANT

Dana G. Kurfman is Social Studies Supervisor for Prince Georges County Public Schools, Maryland, and has served in a similar capacity for the Ann Arbor Public Schools, Michigan. He has been a social studies department chairman for the Educational Testing Service, and was editor of *Evaluation in Geographic Education,* the National Council for Geographic Education Yearbook.

GEOGRAPHY CONSULTANT

A. David Hill is Professor of Geography and Chairman of the Council on Learning and Teaching of the University of Colorado. He is a participant in a number of national panels and institutes, including the Advisory Board of the Center for Education in the Social Sciences at the University of Colorado.

HISTORY CONSULTANT

Martin Ridge, Professor of American History at Indiana University, is managing editor of the *Journal of American History.* In addition to receiving a Guggenheim Fellowship, he has been a William Randolph Hearst Fellow; a Fellow of the Huntington Library, Pasadena, California; and a Fellow of the American Council of Learned Societies.

TEACHER CONSULTANT

Sally Kitano
*North Hill Elementary School
Seattle, Washington*

EDITORIAL ADVISER

Howard D. Mehlinger, Editorial Adviser for the Houghton Mifflin Social Studies programs, is Professor of History and Education at Indiana University. He has been a teacher and a social studies department chairman in Lawrence, Kansas.

CONTENTS

2 WHAT IS A HUMAN BEING?

3 WHAT ARE GROUPS?

4 WHO AM I?

MAPS AND CHARTS

WHO ARE WE?

WINDOWS ON OUR WORLD

THE HOUGHTON MIFFLIN SOCIAL STUDIES PROGRAM

Who Are You?

This is me. Can you guess who I am?

This is my home. Is this your home?

Here are some things I do. Do you do the same things?

I work and play with others. Do you?

I am me.
Who are you?
I live on Earth.
Do you too?

I am me.
Who are you?
I eat and drink.
Do you too?

I am me.
Who are you?
I use tools.
Do you too?

I am me.
Who are you?
I talk and write.
Do you too?

I am me.
Who are you?
I live with others.
Do you too?

I am me.
Who are you?
We are alike,
But different too!

There is no one just like me.
Is there anyone just like you?

"I'm Carol's father."

"I'm the TV repairman."

Who are you? "That's easy," you say. "I have a name. That tells who I am." But sometimes it isn't so easy.

In each of these pictures, someone is answering the question, "Who are you?" But they aren't saying their names. Can you explain the answer each one is giving?

Look at their answers. Are any of the answers true for you as well as for the person in the picture? Which ones? Are the answers true for other members of your class? Are they true for everybody in the world?

"I'm the new shortstop."

"I'm an American."

How many ways could you answer the question, "Who are you?"

Some answers are true for just one person. "I am Robin Snyder from Grant School." Some answers are true for several people. "I am a Cub Scout in Pack 247." Some answers are true for many, many people. "I am an American." And some answers are true for everyone in the world. Can you think of some answers that are true for everybody?

Who are you? This book is about the answers that are true for everybody.

"I'm a human being."

WHAT IS EARTH?

People have always wondered about Earth. They've wondered about its neighbors, too. What does Earth mean to you? What do you think of Earth's neighbors?

WONDERING
ABOUT EARTH

What is Earth?
Is it the tail of a dragon?
Is it the head of a troll?
Is it the hump of a camel?
Or the nose of a mole?

Where is Earth?
Is it on top of a hill?
Is it in a pelican's bill?
Is it on an elephant's back?
Or on a railroad track?

What does Earth do?
Does it swing like a clock?
Does it sit like a rock?
Does it spin like a top?
Does it move? Does it stop?

What holds Earth up?
Does a little white pup?
Does a bowl or a cup?
Does it hang from the moon?
Or a fancy balloon?

What shape is Earth?
Is it flat like a pie?
Is it square like a die?
Is it shaped like an egg?
Or long like a peg?

Can you answer any of these questions?
What do you think Earth is? What questions
have you ever asked about Earth?
People long ago wondered about Earth. What
do you think they said?

WHAT DID PEOPLE THINK ABOUT EARTH?

You aren't the first person to ask questions about Earth. People began to wonder about Earth as soon as they could wonder about anything at all. Earth was important to people long ago, because Earth was their home. Earth still is important to us, because it still is our home.

For a long time people have asked, "What is Earth?" People all asked the same question, but they did not all give the same answer.

A long time ago, people in India asked, "What is Earth?" They thought of an answer. Here is

what people in India thought about Earth.

Earth is like a big, flat plate. Over Earth hangs a roof like a big bowl. The sun, moon, and stars are attached to the roof. They move across the roof above Earth.

Other people had different ideas. Greece is far away from India. But people in Greece asked the same question as people in India. "What is Earth?"

WHAT THE EARLY MEXICANS THOUGHT

This early Mexican priest is telling a tale about Earth. The early Mexicans thought of Earth this way. Compare their ideas about Earth with yours.

One famous Greek teacher was named **Anaximenes** (an-ak-SIM'-eh-neez). Anaximenes thought about Earth. Here is his idea.

Earth is flat like a table. It hangs in the air. Water from rivers and lakes rises through the air. The water gets thinner and thinner as it goes higher and higher. When it is very thin and very high, the water suddenly changes to fire! That is how stars are made.

Anaxagoras (an-ak-SAG'uh-rus), another teacher in Greece, had a different idea about Earth. Here is his idea.

Earth is a huge spinning ball. As Earth spins around, large stones fly off into space. As the stones travel, they get hotter and hotter. The stones get so hot that they start to shine. The biggest stone that flew off long ago became the sun. A smaller one became the moon. The littlest stones became stars.

Not everyone liked these ideas. Some people in those days thought the sun and moon were gods. These people were very angry when Anaxagoras said their gods were just hot stones! They were so angry that they sent Anaxagoras away from their city.

Suppose you had been one of those people. How would you have felt? Have you ever been angry when someone said you were wrong? Have other people been angry when you said they were wrong? What happened?

People have thought of many other answers to the question, "What is Earth?" These drawings show some different ideas about Earth. Can you explain them?

26

Have you ever been anywhere where you could see this far in all directions? What happens where the sky and the land come together? What shape does Earth look like in this picture? Is it the same shape as a table? A dinner plate? A ball?

If you watched the **astronauts** (AS'truh-nawts) on television, you may have seen pictures of Earth from very far away. Or if you have been in an airplane, then you have seen far across Earth. But for thousands of years there were no airplanes or astronauts. Because no one could see more of Earth than this picture shows, most people thought Earth was flat.

A few people believed Earth was round like a ball. Some of these people were sailors. They had noticed a strange thing. Pretend you are a sailor watching for other ships. Look at these pictures. What happens as another ship gets closer and closer to you? Does this tell you anything about the shape of Earth?

Some brave **explorers** (ek-SPLOR'urz) decided to try to sail all the way around Earth. Other people were afraid of such a thought. Why do you think they were afraid?

The explorers set out in their ships. They sailed for months and months. They kept going in the same direction. At last they came back to the place where they had started. (You can try this. Use the globe and a toy boat.) What did the explorers prove about the shape of Earth?

It was hard for people to believe that you could go all the way around Earth. It was hard to believe Earth was round like a ball. After all, Earth does not look round. But the explorers' trips could not be explained any other way.

After these trips, people *knew* that Earth was round. But they still could not *see* that Earth was round. Today, astronauts can see that Earth is round. The pictures on the next page show how Earth looks to an astronaut. What is happening in these pictures?

Why did people first think Earth was flat?
What made them change their minds?
When we are on Earth, why can't we see what shape it is?
What shape is Earth?

WHERE IS EARTH?

Do you wake up just as soon as it is light out? If you do, you might see the sun as it looks in the first picture. What do you call that time of day? How does the sun look?

What time of day is it in the other pictures?
What seems to happen to the sun from one picture
to the next?

Find the sun, moon, and stars in this drawing. What are they moving around? What seems to be the most important thing in the picture?

For hundreds of years, people have watched the sun. From morning to night, the sun seems to move across the sky. But Earth seems to stand still. So people once believed the sun moved around Earth. This drawing shows where people thought Earth was.

There were several reasons why people thought Earth was the center of everything. You have already discovered one important reason. What is it?

Another reason came from the way people felt about themselves. The drawing below gives you a hint. How do you think the man in the picture feels about himself? How do you think he feels about all the other things around him? Which seems more important in this picture, Earth or the sun? Earth or the stars?

How does this drawing help to explain why people thought Earth was the center of everything?

Draw a picture of yourself doing something you usually do in the morning. Draw other pictures of things you usually do at noon or in the afternoon. Show what time it is in your pictures by showing where the sun is.

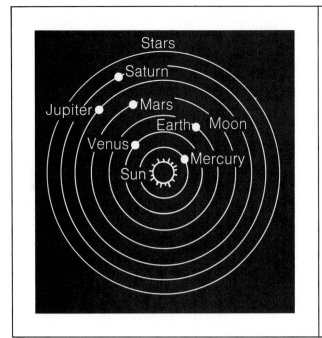
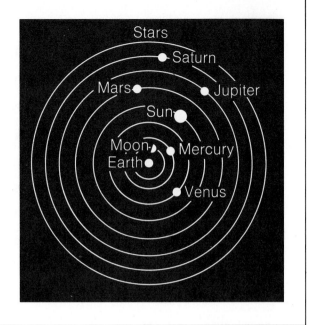

DOES EARTH MOVE?

About four hundred years ago, a scientist named **Copernicus** (ko-PUR'nik-us) wrote a book. Copernicus said Earth is *not* the center of everything. He said Earth moves around the sun. How is that different from what people thought before? Which picture shows Copernicus's idea? Which one shows what people thought before?

Copernicus said Earth is a **planet.** Planets move around the sun. Do you know the names of some other planets besides Earth?

You can see some of the planets in the sky at night. Planets may look like stars to you, but they are different. Both pictures on the next page show the same group of stars. This group of stars is called Leo. Do you see the new "star" in the second picture? It isn't a star at all! It is the planet Venus. It moved into Leo's part of the sky after the first picture was taken. Planets are sometimes in one part of the sky, sometimes in another.

At first only a few people heard about Copernicus's new ideas. But slowly more and more people began to read his book. Earth moves around the sun! It was an exciting idea, but it made some people angry.

About one hundred years after Copernicus died, a scientist named **Galileo** (gal-i-LAY'oh) made more discoveries. He began to think Copernicus had been right. And then people became angry at Galileo. Some people were so angry that Galileo was arrested. He was taken to a judge for trial.

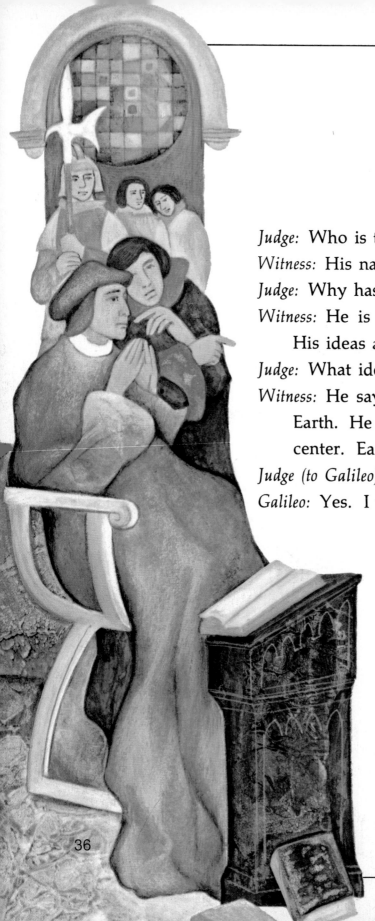

Galileo's Trial

Judge: Who is this man?

Witness: His name is Galileo.

Judge: Why has he been arrested?

Witness: He is teaching ideas that are not true. His ideas are wrong and dangerous.

Judge: What ideas is he teaching?

Witness: He says the sun does not move around Earth. He says instead that the sun is in the center. Earth moves around the sun.

Judge (to Galileo): Did you really say that?

Galileo: Yes. I think it's true.

Judge: I do not feel Earth moving. Neither does anyone else. Where did you get such a strange idea?

Galileo: For many years I have studied the stars with a telescope.

Judge: And what is a telescope?

Galileo: It is a new tool. A telescope makes things look closer and bigger. With a telescope you can see things that are very far away.

Witness: What difference does a telescope make? All the books say Earth is the center of everything. The people who wrote the books were wise. You should listen to them, Galileo.

Judge: How did your telescope give you these strange ideas?

Galileo: With the telescope, I can see the moon and stars and planets very well. All the planets move around the sun.

Judge: What does all this have to do with Earth?

Galileo: I think Earth is a planet, too. If that is true, Earth must move around the sun.

Judge: Earth is a planet? Just another planet? An ordinary planet? Not the center of everything? Nonsense! It can't be true.

Witness: See what I told you? He thinks Earth is just a planet. The man is crazy!

Judge: Galileo, we can't have you teaching this nonsense. Your punishment is to go home and stay there as long as you live. Never leave your house. That way, no one will hear these foolish ideas.

Do you think people forgot about Galileo's ideas after the judge sent him home?

Looking at Pictures

1. Look at the pictures on pages 22 and 25. How are these ideas of Earth the same? How are they different?

2. Look at the pictures on page 34. Explain the ideas about Earth that each picture shows.

3. Find a picture between pages 20 and 37 that shows the correct shape of Earth. How do you know this picture is correct?

4. What pictures between pages 20 and 37 show why people thought Earth was flat?

5. Look at the pictures on pages 30 and 31. Which shows your favorite time of day? Why?

What Do You Think?

6. Write a story about the picture on page 33. Use this sentence as the beginning of your story. Complete the story any way you want:

    There once was a king who believed he was at the center of everything in the heavens.

7. Pretend you are the judge at Galileo's trial. What would you say to Galileo about his ideas of Earth? Would you punish him?

8. Do you think that humans are more important than Earth? Why?

HOW IS EARTH LIKE A SPACESHIP?

You have read how some people in the past described Earth. Some said Earth was like a flat table. Can you remember other things people said about Earth?

Some people today describe Earth another way. They say, "Earth is a spaceship." Do you think of yourself as a passenger on a spaceship? Probably not. But in many ways, Earth *is* like a spaceship.

For one thing, Earth travels through space. You ride on Earth as it travels. Spaceship Earth carries you from day to night.

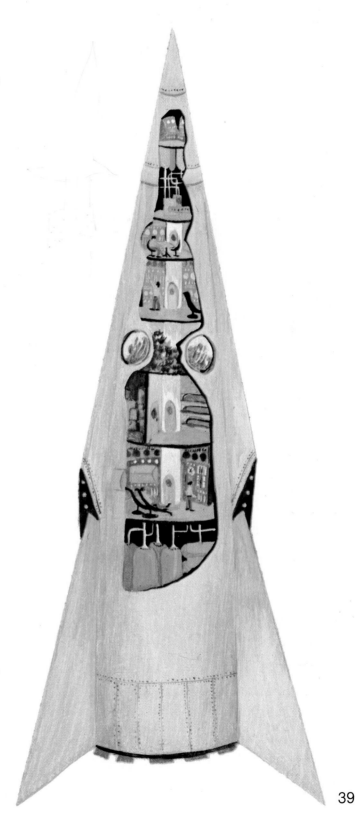

At the edge of the world
It is growing light.
The trees stand shining.
I like it.
It is growing light.

In the evening glow
The wind gathers
The chattering birds.
It is time to go to bed.

How do you feel about day? How do you feel about night? What do you do during the day? What do you do during the night?

What causes day and night? People have had many ideas about the cause. How does this picture explain day and night?

Copernicus and Galileo showed people that the sun did not go around Earth. There has to be another reason for day and night. Here is a picture of Earth. This is how Earth looks from space. What is the difference between side A and side B?

The sun's light cannot shine on the whole Earth at once. Earth has a shadow, just as you do. Part of Earth is in a shadow. Is it day or night on side A?

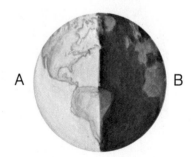

A   B

How does spaceship Earth carry you from day to night?

41

Earth spins like a top. Earth spins in space. Another word for spin is **rotate**. Earth rotates in space. Earth takes 24 hours to make one full turn. One full turn is called a **rotation**.

As Earth rotates, it carries you into the sun's light. Then it is daytime. Earth continues to turn. It carries you away from the sun's light. You are in the shadow. Then it is night.

Lin is a child your age who lives in China. China is on the other side of Earth. In picture 1, would you be awake or asleep? Would Lin be awake or asleep? In picture 2, who would be awake? Who would be asleep? Explain how you move from the night side to the day side.

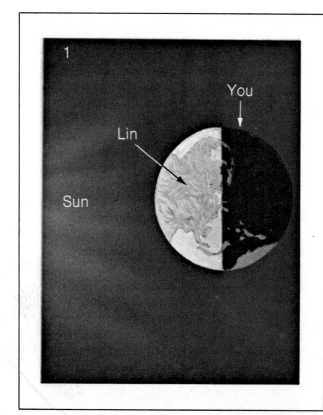

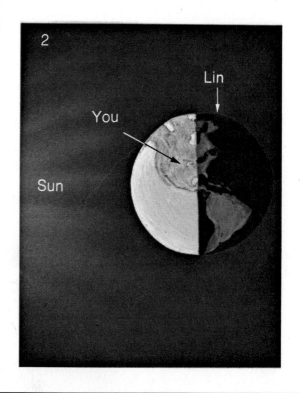

WHERE DOES EARTH GO?

Earth is always moving. It rotates to give you day and night. And it moves through space in another way, too. What did Copernicus say about Earth's movement?

Spaceship Earth always travels the same path. Its path goes around the sun. How long does Earth take to go all the way around the sun? Here is a hint. On your last birthday, Earth was at one particular spot on its journey. On your next birthday, it will be back at the same spot. How many times have you gone around the sun since you were born?

The pictures on the next two pages show the changes you see in one year's trip around the sun. What are these changes called?

The Seasons

What are two ways Earth moves?
How long does it take Earth to rotate once?
How long does it take Earth to go around
the sun one time?

How do these changes affect people's lives?

In what season is your birthday? Draw a picture of something you do in that season. Show some signs of the season. Let the class guess the season in your picture.

45

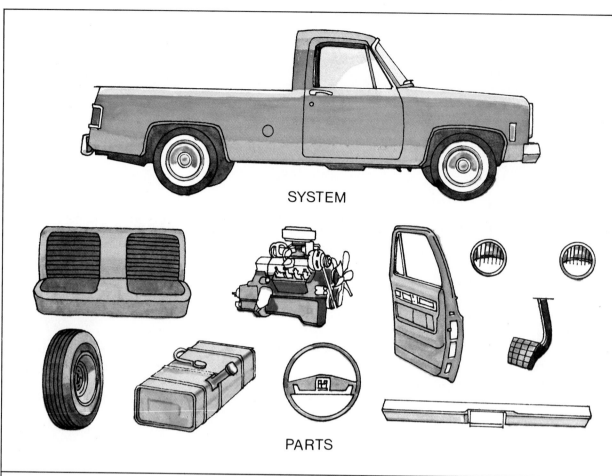

SYSTEM

PARTS

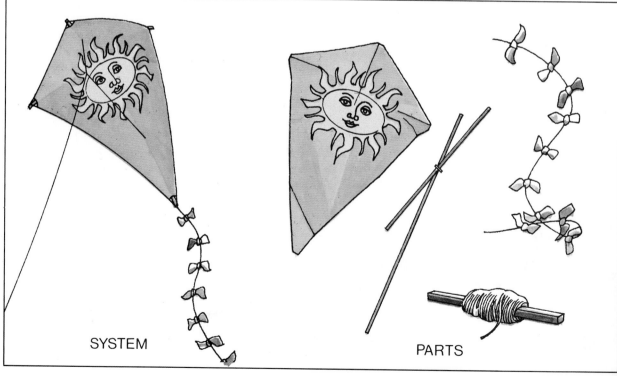

SYSTEM

PARTS

WHAT IS A SYSTEM?

A spaceship is a **system** (SIS'tum). A system? What's that? It's not some special secret machine that only astronauts can use. There are many different kinds of systems. You use some systems every day.

A system is made up of several parts. The parts of a system work together. The parts need each other to work. On page 46 are pictures of two systems.

What does the first system do? What does the second system do? What do you call a system that tells time? What other systems are in your classroom? What does each one do?

A spaceship has several different systems. The rocket system keeps the spaceship moving. The camera system takes pictures to send back to Earth.

Spaceships that carry people need a special system. This system keeps the passengers alive. It is called the **life-support system.** Some things you saw in the spaceship on page 39 were parts of the life support system.

Spaceship Earth has passengers. Spaceship Earth keeps its passengers alive. So Spaceship Earth must have a life support system. What parts make up Earth's life support system?

I'm inside balloons and bubbles.

If you leave Earth, you must take me along.

You can't see me, but you can see what I do. What am I?

WHAT KEEPS YOU ALIVE?

Most of the time, you don't even think about air. But you breathe several times every minute, even when you're sitting still. When you are running, you breathe faster. You use a lot of air!

What is air? Why is it so important for you? Air is a **mixture**. Have you ever stirred chocolate into your milk? That is a mixture. Can you think of some other mixtures?

One important part of the air mixture is **oxygen** (AHK'suh-jun). Your body needs oxygen. That is why you can only hold your breath for a little while. You take oxygen from the air when you breathe *in*. All living things need oxygen.

Another part of the air mixture is **carbon dioxide**. You put carbon dioxide into the air when you breathe *out*.

You may have noticed a problem. All living things breathe in oxygen. All living things breathe out carbon dioxide. Why isn't the oxygen all used up?

Green plants breathe in oxygen, just like every other living thing. But they do something else, too. During the day, green plants use carbon dioxide to make their food. And they put oxygen back into the air. All the oxygen you breathe comes from green plants. Some are giant trees.

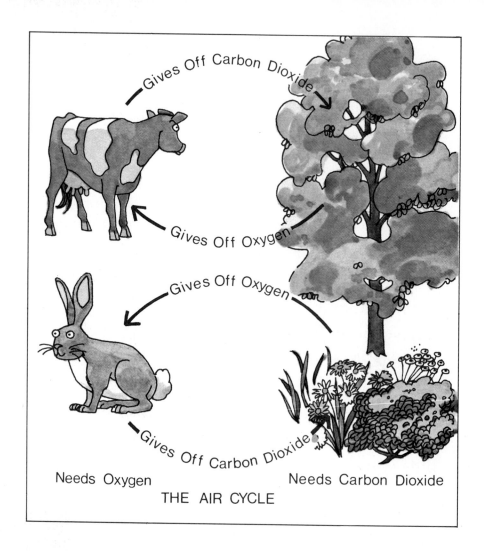

Gives Off Carbon Dioxide

Gives Off Oxygen

Gives Off Oxygen

Gives Off Carbon Dioxide

Needs Oxygen

Needs Carbon Dioxide

THE AIR CYCLE

Some are tiny ocean plants. Have you thanked a green plant today?

Is air part of Earth's life support system?
How do you know?
How do plants help you?
How do you help plants?

ANOTHER PART
OF THE
LIFE-SUPPORT SYSTEM

I'm in the air.
I'm on the ground.
There's hardly anywhere
I can't be found.

When I'm cold,
I'm hard and clear.
If I get too hot,
I disappear!

You call me clouds
When I'm wet and gray.
When I'm fluffy white,
It's a snowy day.

From the world map
You can clearly see,
Most of Earth
Is covered by me!

What am I?

How often every day do you drink water? What other things besides water do you drink when you are thirsty? Milk, juice, and soda all have water in them. Fruits and vegetables have water in them, too. So you drink a lot more water than you thought you did. In fact, you need water more often than you need food.

How many ways do you use water besides drinking it?

Water takes many different forms. All the pictures here show water. What name do you have for the water in each picture?

You saw that plants and animals use the same air over and over again. Each one puts in what the other needs. Otherwise, the air would be used up.

Water is used over and over again, too. Rain falls from the clouds into rivers and oceans. But water **evaporates** (ih-VAP'uh-rates) from rivers and oceans. The evaporated water makes new clouds in the sky. Is water part of Earth's life support system? How do you know?

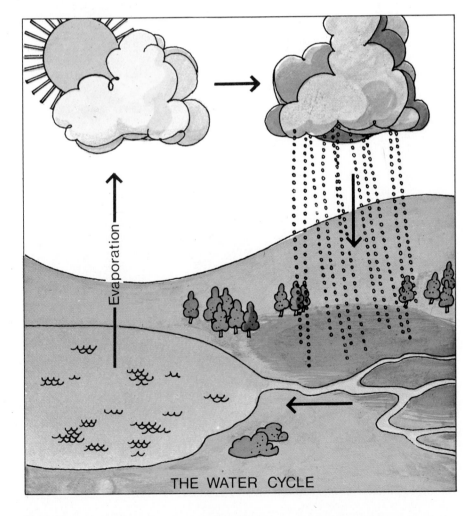

THE WATER CYCLE

WHERE DO YOU GET YOUR FOOD?

All living things need food. Earth's life-support system lets living things get the food they need.

Plants need sunlight to make food. They take carbon dioxide from the air. What puts the carbon dioxide into the air? Plants use minerals and water from the **soil,** too. The soil is very important for plants. Their roots grow deep into the soil to find water and other things they need. Make a list of everything a plant uses to make food.

Animals do not make their own food the way plants do. What are the animals in the first picture eating? What foods do people eat that are shown in the picture?

What kind of food does the fox eat? Does the fox need plants to stay alive?

Some animals eat nothing but plants to stay alive. Other animals eat nothing but meat. The meat-eaters hunt the plant-eaters. Do the meat-eaters need plants to stay alive? Some animals eat both plants and meat. What kinds of food are the bears eating?

Make a list of the kinds of food you eat in a day. In which group do human beings belong?

This system of getting food is called the **food chain.** Each link in the food chain is fastened to another. Plants are the beginning of the food chain. The corn grows. The chicken eats the corn. The fox eats the chicken.

Soil

Dead Plants

Look at the picture above. How do the plants get their food? Which animals eat plants? Which ones eat meat?

How many links are there in the food chain that ends with the cat? Write them down. What are the links in the food chain that ends with the person?

Why do you think this system is called a food chain? Why do all animals need plants, whether they are plant-eaters or not?

WHAT KEEPS YOUR SPACESHIP GOING?

A spaceship needs **energy**. Energy is what makes things work. A spaceship needs energy to travel. It needs energy to keep the life support system working. Energy keeps all parts of the system working together. Without energy, the system slows down and stops.

Think of some systems. Where does the energy for each one come from?

Where does spaceship Earth get the energy for its life-support system? There is *one* thing that is needed in *all* parts of the system.

It keeps water evaporating to make new clouds. *It* keeps plants growing to become food. Plants need *it* to make oxygen, too. *It* is where Earth gets energy. Can you guess what *it* is?

Earth's energy comes from the sun. Without the sun, all parts of Earth's life-support system would stop working.

The sun gives Earth light and heat. These are two kinds of energy. When does Earth get more of the sun's energy, in summer or in winter?

On Earth, the sun's energy is changed. Green plants use the energy to grow. The sun's energy becomes leaves, fruit, roots. The energy is kept in the plant. The energy stays there until it is used.

Some of the sun's energy was kept in this seed. Now it is being used. What is using the energy?

What is using the sun's energy in each of these pictures?

Can you explain how this child is getting energy from the sun?

USING THINGS OVER

There are problems with living on a spaceship. There is not much room. There is not enough room to carry big tanks of water. Astronauts must take just enough water and use it over and over again. Machines clean the water so it can be used many times. When you use something over instead of throwing it away, you have **recycled** (ree-SY′kuld) it.

Even on a spaceship as big as Earth, recycling is important. Just like the astronauts, we must use things over. Then there will be enough for our long trip through space.

There is something you use every day that can be recycled. Paper! Paper is made from wood. People cut down trees and take the wood to a paper mill. At the mill, the wood is made into paper.

People need trees for other things, too. Remember that trees are plants. Trees help make oxygen. And wood for houses comes from trees. What other ways do we use trees and their wood?

There are not enough trees to make all the houses and all the paper and all the parks we would like to have. When there is not enough of something, we say it is **scarce**. Trees are scarce. That means there are not enough trees for everything we want. So we must decide what we need most. Can you think of other things that are scarce?

When something is scarce, it is important to recycle it. Paper can be recycled. New paper can be made from old paper. How would recycling paper save trees?

What will happen to this tree?

Other things can be recycled, too. Here are two things people use every day. What do you do with them when you are finished? Use the pictures to tell what happens after you throw a bottle away.

What can you do with the bottle instead of throwing it away?

Why is it a good idea to recycle things?

63

LIVING ON A SPACESHIP

How does your spaceship move?

To live on a spaceship, you have to plan carefully. You must be sure to have all the things you need. There must be enough of everything for all the people on the trip. There is not enough room on the spaceship for everything you might want. You have to choose carefully.

What keeps you alive on your spaceship?

Pretend your class is going on a trip into space. The trip will last for the rest of your life. What must you take to stay alive? What things should you take to stay healthy and happy? How can you make sure that you don't run out of things you need?

68

Looking at Pictures

1. Look at these drawings at left. Why is each of these a system?

2. Look at the picture below. What part of the life support system is *not* shown in the picture?

3. The pictures on page 54 show some meat-eaters and plant-eaters. Draw a food chain using some of these plants and animals.

What Do You Think?

4. Earth goes around the sun. Draw pictures showing what happens when Earth is in each of the four different places around the sun.

5. List some of the objects you use at home and in school. Which of these could be recycled when they are old?

6. What might Earth be like if it did not rotate?

WHAT IS AROUND EARTH?

Have you noticed that you can't talk about Earth without talking about Earth's neighbors, too? For example, the sun. You couldn't say much about Earth without saying something about the sun, too.

People who study Earth's neighbors are called **astronomers** (uh-STRON'uh-murs). Galileo, Copernicus, Anaxagoras, Anaximenes — all were astronomers. Astronomers find out all they can about everything in the sky.

Here are some ways astronomers have studied the moon. Which is the oldest way? Which is the newest way?

The moon is the only one of Earth's neighbors that humans have visited. That is because the moon is Earth's nearest neighbor.

WHAT THE MOON SAID

Of all the things
    in the evening sky,
none is so close
    to Earth as I!

My trip around Earth
    every 28 days
changes my face
    in several ways.

At night the sun
    gives you no light.
I do my best,
    but I'm not as bright.

I have no light
    of my own, you see.
I only give back
    what the sun gives me.

Look at the two pictures. Where does the light come from that makes the shadow?

WHICH IS BETTER, THE SUN OR THE MOON?

Once a friend asked the wise man, "Which is better, the sun or the moon?"

"The moon is better, of course," said the wise man.

"Why do you think so?" asked the friend.

"Look," replied the wise man, "the sun comes out in the daytime when we don't really need it, since it's always bright then anyway. However, if it weren't for the moon, it would be pitch dark everywhere at night."

What is wrong with the wise man's answer?
Does he really seem to be a wise man?

WHAT ARE THE OTHER PLANETS?

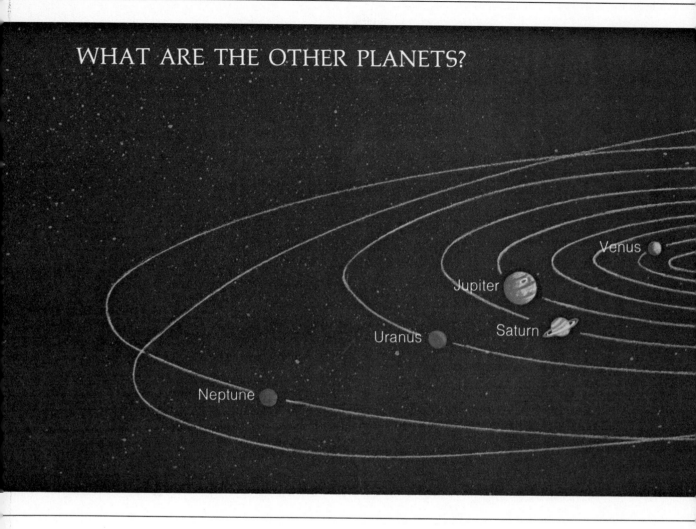

Earth is a planet, and Earth travels around the sun. There are other planets which also travel around the sun. Look at this picture. How many planets go around the sun? What can you tell about each planet?

This group of planets travels around the sun. The sun is larger than any of the planets. In fact, the sun is the most important part of this picture. The sun and the planets together are called the **solar system**. *Sol* is another name for the sun.

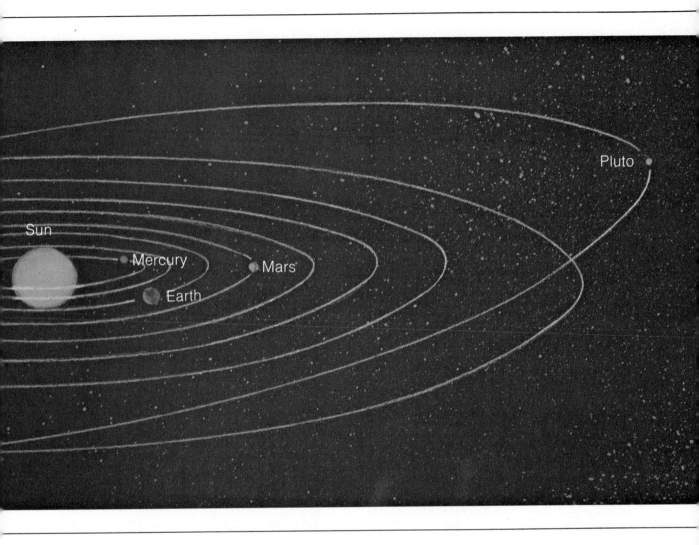

So "solar system" just means "the sun's system." What are the parts of the solar system?

In Galileo's time, people only knew of the six planets nearest the sun. Uranus, Neptune, and Pluto were too far away to be seen easily, even with telescopes. The first people who saw these planets thought they were dim stars. Many scientists now think there may be another planet somewhere beyond Pluto. There are still many mysteries about the solar system.

DOES ANYONE ELSE LIVE HERE?

SATURN

VENUS

MARS

JUPITER

All the planets are like spaceships traveling around the sun. Spaceship Earth carries some passengers. Earth has a special life-support system to keep the passengers alive. Do any of the other planets carry passengers?

This chart tells you some things about the planets. First, list the parts of Earth's life-support system. Now look at the chart. Does any planet besides Earth have all the parts of the life-support system? Do any planets seem to be too hot or too cold for people and animals? Do you think there are living things like us on any of the other planets?

	Is there water?	Is there carbon dioxide?	Is there oxygen?	How hot or cold?
Mercury	no	no	no	750° above zero
Venus	maybe	yes	no	800° above zero
Earth	yes	yes	yes	120° below zero to 136° above zero
Mars	yes	yes	no	50° below zero to 90° above zero
Jupiter	maybe	no	no	240° below zero
Saturn	maybe	no	no	285° below zero
Uranus	maybe	no	no	325° below zero
Neptune	maybe	no	no	365° below zero
Pluto	?	?	?	380° below zero

IS ANYONE OUT THERE?

Humans have explored the solar system with telescopes. Astronauts have landed on the moon. Space probes have traveled to Mercury, Venus, Mars, and Jupiter. With telescopes and probes, people on Earth have learned that no one else lives in the solar system. There are no passengers like you on the other spaceships. If anything lives on the other planets at all, it could only be something like a very tiny plant. Does that mean there are no other living things like us anywhere? Where else can people look for other living things?

Do you know what a star is? Stars look tiny because they are very far away. They are even farther away than the planets. But *one* star does

not look tiny. *One* star is much closer than all the others. That star is the sun! Our sun is a star. And all the stars you see at night are faraway suns.

Our sun is part of a group of stars called the Milky Way. The picture above shows what the Milky Way looks like. The arrow points to our sun. Beyond the Milky Way are other groups of stars.

Millions and millions of suns! Do some of these suns have planets moving around them? Astronomers are sure that other suns do have planets. But these planets are too far away for us to see, even with the most powerful telescopes. There are so many suns and so many planets that scientists are almost sure there are some planets like Earth. There are probably many planets with air, water, soil, and sunlight. If a planet is very much like Earth, then living things there might be very much like living things here. But living things on another planet might be different, too. They might be a little bit different or they might be *very* different. What do you think?

How do you think people from another solar system would look? Draw a picture of them. Do you think they are very different from us? If they are, how can we call them "people"? What might they call themselves? What might they call us? Write a story about life on another planet.

Looking at Pictures

1. Turn to the pictures on page 69. What kind of work do astronomers do?
2. Look at the pictures of the moon and Earth on page 70. In what ways are the moon and Earth alike? In what ways are they different?
3. Write the names of the planets in the order of their distance from the sun. Which planet is closest to the sun? Which is farthest away? Use the picture on pages 72 and 73 to help you write your list.
4. Study the chart on page 75. Look at the information of one column, such as *Is there water?*. Tell why each planet could or could not support life.

What Do You Think?

5. Are there planets in our solar system that are farther away than Pluto? Why do you think that we do not know?
6. Why do you think human beings are so interested in space travel?
7. Would you like to travel to another planet? Why or why not? What would you look for if you did go? What would you expect? What might you be afraid of? What might please you about the planet?
8. Turn to the pictures on page 74. Pick one of the planets shown. Pretend there is life on that planet. Tell what that life is like.

1. Suppose you become an astronaut when you grow up. From your space trips you discover that Earth is *not* really part of the solar system. Think about what happened to Galileo. How do you think people might feel about your discovery?

2. We have learned about Earth and the solar system from astronomers and astronauts. Have your teacher point out on a globe the homes of these people. What does this show?

3. *Food, water,* and *air* are three parts of the life-support system. List them in order of their importance to your life. What does your list show you?

4. Look at the pictures on this page. Change their numbers to show how plants bring you energy from the sun. Write a story explaining how the sun helps you to live and grow. Use the pictures to help you.

5. Suppose we discovered people on other planets with whom we could talk. What would you say to them? What would you want to know from them?

UNIT 2

WHAT IS A HUMAN BEING?

What makes you human?
Is it the way you walk or the way you talk? Is it
the hair on your head or the way you get fed?

Humans live on Earth with many other living
things. How are humans like other living things?
How are they different?

JANE AND MARK

Faces of Me

OLU

I looked through my picture book
To see what I could see.
I saw a lot of faces
Staring back at me.

I saw
    Jane and Mark
    Carlos and Soong
    Olu and Choon.

CARLOS

CHOON

YAFFA

HEIKO

KIGTAG

I saw
> Yaffa and Heiko
> Kigtag and Nico
> Sayed and Hedda.

All of them are human beings,
People, don't you see?
The faces in my picture book
Are all faces of me.

SAYED

HEDDA

83

How many living things can this child see? Living things are all around. Look around your classroom. What living things do you see? Now look out the window. Name the living things you can see outside. How did you decide what belonged on your list?

MANY KINDS OF LIVING THINGS

Living things are everywhere. They are under the ground, in the air, in the oceans, on top of high mountains. Can you think of a living thing you might find in each of these places?

Living things come in all sizes. Some are so tiny you can't see them without a microscope. In a drop of water, there are many living things. Other living things are huge. What do you think is the biggest living thing?

Even though living things are so different, they are all alike in some ways. You are a living thing, too. How are you like other living things?

Living things come in all shapes and colors.

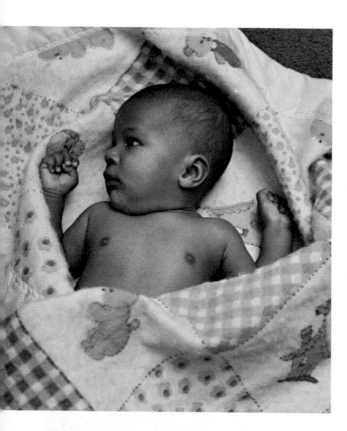

ALL LIVING THINGS
ARE BORN AND GROW

LEAVING COPIES

A cat will have a baby cat,
Never, never a baby bat.
A bear will have a baby bear,
Never, never a baby hare.
A bee will have a baby bee,
Never, never a baby flea.
A whale will have a baby whale,
Never, never a baby snail.
An eagle will have a baby eagle,
Never, never a baby beagle.
A swan will have a baby swan,
Never, never a baby fawn.
A monkey will have a baby
monkey,
Never, never a baby donkey.
A moose will have a baby
moose,
Never, never a baby goose.

87

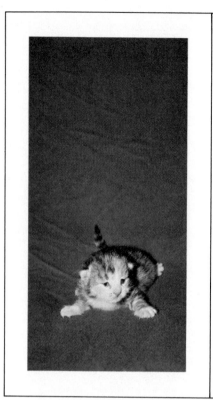  

Every living thing comes from another living thing of the same kind. All living things are born. After they are born, young living things change. What is happening in these pictures?

All living things grow. The kitten grew into a cat. How did it change as it grew? You can tell that a kitten will be a cat. But some living things change completely as they grow. The butterfly looks very different from the caterpillar.

You are growing, too. You grow every day. Can you tell ways you have grown?

HOW DO I KNOW I'M GROWING?

I can't wear last year's coat. It's too tight.
Last year's shoes are too small for me.
My legs are too long to ride my old tricycle.
Now I can reach the shelf for the peanut butter.
I don't have to stand on a chair any more.
I can carry a whole bag of groceries.
I can even pick up my baby brother.
I can kick the ball farther.
I can run faster.
I can jump higher.
I can play longer.
With all these clues, I know I'm growing.
What clues tell you that you are growing?

ALL LIVING THINGS DIE

Mary Ellis

Mary Ellis was my dog. She was so big I could ride on her back. We had Mary Ellis for as long as I could remember. She was part of our family.

90

One evening, Mary Ellis would not eat. Mother said she might be sick.

The next morning I went to Mary Ellis. She did not move. She lay very still. "Mother, come quick," I called.

Mother came and looked. "Mary Ellis is dead," she said quietly.

"Dead?" I repeated, and I started to cry.

"Don't cry," Mother said. "Mary Ellis had a long life."

"But I will miss her," I said, still crying.

"So will I," said Mother.

Just as all living things are born and grow, all living things die. Life must come to an end. A flower, a bee, a tree, a dog, and even you will die. Everything that is alive will die someday.

What do you suppose would happen if all the fish in the sea lived forever? Suppose no fish ever died. Draw a picture showing how the sea would look.

WHAT DO LIVING THINGS NEED?

You are a passenger on spaceship Earth, remember? All other living things are passengers, too. All living things share the life-support system on spaceship Earth. All living things have other needs, too. Look at these pictures. What do all living things need?

WHAT KEEPS LIVING THINGS SAFE?

Living things *protect* themselves from danger. They must protect themselves to stay alive. They protect themselves from sickness, from hunger, and from other living things.

Some living things are protected by the way they are made. What protects this cactus from being eaten? What protects the porcupine?

Other living things are protected by things they do. Some birds fly south in the winter to protect themselves from cold and hunger.

Most animals do not think about protecting themselves. They protect themselves without thinking, by **instinct** (IN'stingt). Instinct is something you are born knowing. Birds fly south by instinct. Squirrels climb trees by instinct.

How are the animals on the next page protecting themselves?

Some animals protect each other, too. How is the mother lion protecting her cub?

Human beings need to be protected, too. How do you protect yourself from cold? From sickness? Can you think of ways that other people help protect you? Name some of these people. How does your house protect you?

Do you have to think about protection? Do people build houses by instinct, or do they have to learn to build houses?

What are some things that protect you at home? At school? In a car? Are there times when you help to protect other people? How are the people in these pictures being protected?

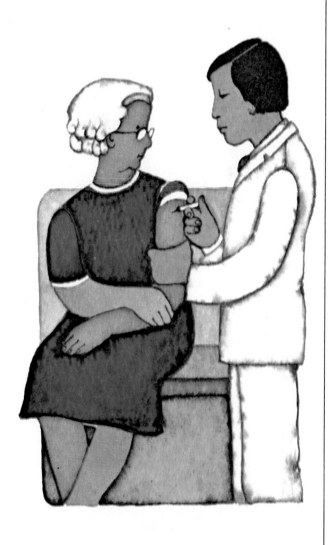

Looking at Pictures

1. Look at the pictures on page 88. What happens to *all* living things? Now look at the pictures on pages 92 and 93. What needs do living things have? How are *all* living things alike?

2. What happens to humans as they grow? Look at the pictures at left to help you answer the question.

3. Look at the pictures below. What is saving or protecting the child in each picture?

What Do You Think?

4. Have you ever stood under a tree to keep out of the sun or rain? How do humans use other living things?

5. Look at the picture of the dog on page 93. How do you think it feels? What do you think it needs?

6. Why do you think humans need rest?

WHICH IS MOST LIKE YOU?

You probably see a hundred living things around you every day. There are birds, trees, people, insects, dogs, and many others. All these living things are alike in important ways. But they are also different in important ways. Here are two living things. What do you think is the biggest difference between them?

Scientists have divided all living things into two big groups, plants and animals. Living things are grouped together because they are alike in some ways. Can you think of ways most plants are alike? How are plants different from animals?

One big difference between plants and animals is the way they get their food. Do you remember how green plants get their food? How is it different from the ways animals get their food?

Another difference between plants and animals is how they move. Can plants move from place to place by themselves? Do most animals move from place to place? Why do you think animals need to move more than plants?

If all living things are either plants or animals, where do human beings belong? Why did you put them in that group?

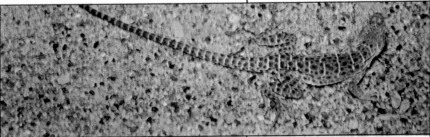

If you said human beings belonged to the animal group, you were right. Human beings are animals, not plants.

But animals are also divided into groups. Humans are more like some of these groups than others. Look at the top row of pictures on page 103. One of these animals is like you in an important way. Which one do you think it is?

Put your hand in the center of your back. Move your hand up and down. Do you feel anything with your fingers? How does it feel? What you feel is your *backbone*. Human beings are animals with backbones. Which of the animals in the first row of pictures has a backbone? There are other ways that you are like that animal with the backbone. What are they?

All the animals in the second row have backbones. But there is still one animal which is more like you than the other two are. Which one do you think it is?

Have you ever touched any of these animals? What does a fish have covering its skin? What does a bird have? What does a dog have? Feel the top of your head. Does it feel most like a bird or a dog or a fish?

Dogs belong to a group of animals called **mammals** (MAM'ulz). Human beings belong to this group, too. Human beings are mammals, not fish or birds. Can you think of other ways that mammals are different from fish and birds?

HOW ARE ALL MAMMALS ALIKE?

Human beings are mammals. Mammals are different from other animals in several ways. Here are some ways you can tell if an animal is a mammal or not.

All mammals have fur or hair. Mammals don't have scales like fish or feathers like birds. Name all the animals you can that have hair. They are all mammals.

Which of the animals above is a mammal? The way mammals are born is different from other animals. All mammals are born alive from their mothers, like these guinea pigs. How is the baby bird being born?

Suzanne and Me

I have a cat named Suzanne. She is yellow with white paws. Suzanne is beautiful. She likes to play. We have fun.

One day Suzanne did not want to play. She just dozed on her favorite chair. I dangled a string in front of her. She yawned. I brought out her favorite ball and bounced it up and down. She closed her eyes. After I bounced the ball a few times, she got up and walked away. Then I noticed her tummy. It was all puffed up. She looked as if she had eaten too much.

"That's it," I said. "Suzanne doesn't want to play because she ate too much." But she kept on acting the same way. By the next week her tummy was even bigger than before.

"Where *is* Suzanne getting all that food?" I said to myself. I decided to watch her. All day I watched, but she didn't do anything but sleep.

The next morning she was as fat as ever. And she scratched at me when I tried to play with her.

"It's the food she's eating. Whatever it is, it isn't good for her. It's making her an old meany." I decided to ask Mother about it.

"Mother, are you feeding Suzanne?"

"No," Mother said. "Suzanne is your responsibility. Why do you ask?"

"Suzanne is gaining a lot of weight," I said. "It is making her lazy and mean."

"Oh, Suzanne isn't getting fat from eating too much," said Mother. "She's going to have kittens."

"KITTENS! Baby kittens!" I shouted.

"Yes. The kittens are growing inside Suzanne's body. She won't play because she doesn't feel like it. You'll have to wait until the kittens are born."

I went back to the chair where Suzanne was sleeping. "Gee, Suzanne, you're super! I can't wait to see your kittens."

Mammals feed their babies differently, too. Can human babies eat the same things you eat as soon as they are born? Baby birds and baby fish can. But baby mammals need milk. The kittens in the picture get milk from their mother.

The turtle's mother laid her eggs in the sand and went away. Who will feed the baby turtle? Could a kitten get its own food as soon as it was born? Could a human baby?

Animals care for their babies in different ways. Many animals like fish and frogs never see their babies. The babies are hatched from eggs and must begin to find their own food.

Birds take care of their babies for a few weeks. Then the young birds learn to fly. After that, they must take care of themselves.

Mammals take care of their babies longer than other animals. Many young mammals stay with their parents for several years.

Sometimes only the mothers take care of the babies. Sometimes the mother and the father both look after them. Sometimes a group of mammals lives together. Then they all help to protect the babies.

One reason why mammals take care of their babies so long is that the babies need their mother's milk. Another reason is that these babies take longer to grow up. Many other living things grow up very quickly. They are born knowing most of the things they need to live. What is it called when you are born knowing how to do something? But mammals need to learn more. Young mammals learn from their parents and from other animals in their group.

Young mammals play to learn. They practice things that will help them when they grow up. Running and jumping make them stronger. Have you ever watched a kitten chase a string? What is the kitten practicing? What are these young animals practicing?

109

HOW ARE HUMANS DIFFERENT?

In some ways, human beings are like all other living things. People need food, rest, air, water, and protection.

Human beings are more like some living things than others. People are more like starfish than trees, because people are animals, not plants. People are more like frogs than starfish, because people have backbones. People are more like dogs than frogs, because people are mammals.

But in some ways, human beings are different from all other living things. How are human beings different?

Pick up your pencil and write your name. Put your pencil down. Now make fists of your hands. Keep your fists closed. Pretend they are paws. Now pick up your pencil between your paws and write your name. Which way was easier? Why?

How would a person carry the stick?

Can you touch your right thumb with each of the fingers on your right hand? Try it. No other animal can do that. Nearly everything you do would be different if your hands were different. (Try to pick up a penny or button your jacket without using your thumbs.)

Look at the way each of these living things stands. What is different about the way the human stands? Try standing like each of the living things.

Suppose you stood the way the fox does. How could you carry your books to school? Could you open the school door when you got there? What other problems would you have?

Humans beings can do many things because they can stand up and walk on two feet. What can these children do because they do not need their hands to help them run?

Right now you are using your human hands to hold your book. You are using your human eyes to look at the book. But you are using something else, too.

Other animals could hold the book and look at it. But no other animal could read the book. No other animal could think about the questions. You are using your human brain to read and think.

THE BIRTH OF AN IDEA

A big red apple is on the table. My brain goes into action. Quickly my eyes flash a message:
Person sees apple!
My eyes report to my brain:
Apple red, round, large!
My nose sends a message:
Apple smells good!
My memory calls out:
You like apples! You're always eating them!
Idea! I'm going to eat this apple!
My brain sends messages back:
Get ready for action!

Different messages go to different places:

Arm, reach for apple!

Fingers, close around apple!

Teeth, get ready to bite into apple!

Throat, get ready to swallow!

Deep inside my brain, a message is sent to my stomach:

This is an alert.

Stomach, get ready to receive a bite

of apple!

All this happens within the time it takes my hand to reach for the apple. Wow! My brain works fast.

How does your brain work with the other parts of your body?

Your brain does more than send messages to your body. Human beings can use their brains to think about what they are doing right now. They can think about things they did long ago. And they can use their brains to think about things they have never done or seen. Human beings are probably the only ones who are able to use their brains this way. Have you ever imagined something? You can do that because you are a human being.

How are human beings different from other living things?

WHAT CAN HUMANS DO?

What other living things need food? Why could only a human being get food this way?

What other living things take care of their babies? Could any other living thing take care of its baby this way?

What other living things play? Why could only a human being play this game?

What will this girl put in her knapsack? Why could only a human being do this?

Looking at Pictures

1. Plants and animals are different. Look at the pictures on page 99. How do the coyote and the tulip get food? How does each of them move?

2. Look at the bottom row of pictures on page 103. How are human bodies different from these animals?

3. Humans are mammals. Birds are *not* mammals. These pictures show one difference between mammals and other animals. Which takes longer to grow, humans or birds?

What Do You Think?

4. Turn to the picture on page 112. Imagine you are a dog. Would you be able to play baseball like these children? Why?

5. Write a story about the picture on page 116.

HUMANS   BIRDS

Newborn

Five Months

One Year

117

THE HUMAN WAY OF LIVING

There are several ways that human beings are different from other living things. Our hands are different. The way we stand is different. The way we walk is different. The way we think is different. Together, these differences mean that humans live a different way from all other living things.

Every kind of animal has its own way of living. So does every kind of plant. Each of these birds has its own way of living. How are they alike? How are they different?

What has the person made? What has the bird made? How many other things that people have made can you see in the first picture? How many other things that birds have made can you see in the second picture? Who makes more things?

The man driving the car is lost. So is the puppy. They are both unhappy. How can the man find out which way to go? Can anyone help him? How can the puppy find its way home? Is there anyone in the picture who can help it? What can the person do that the puppy cannot do?

Human beings make a great many things. Some things you make yourself, like a model airplane. Sometimes you buy things that other people have made.

There are clothes and blankets to keep you warm. People made them. There are fans to keep you cool. There are bathtubs and soap to keep you clean. How do other animals stay warm or cool or clean? There are records and radios to give

you music. There are hospitals and medicines to keep you well. No other animal *makes* so many things as humans do.

Humans make more than "things" you can see and touch. People also make words, so they can talk to each other. Using the words on the map, the lost man can find his way. Or he can use words to ask the policeman.

Human beings make a great many more "things." They make "things" like fire departments for protection. They make "things" like schools for learning.

All these "things" that people make are part of the human way of living. This human way of living is called **culture** (KUL'chur). It is culture which makes the human way of living different.

121

HOW DO YOU USE TOOLS?

All living things need water. A plant must wait for rain to fall over the place the plant is growing. An animal can move around and search for water. But each time the animal is thirsty, it must go back to the stream again.

Human beings can use tools to get the water they need. Even a simple tool like a bucket lets people carry water away from the stream. By filling many jars with water, the people in the picture above can live away from the stream without running out of water.

The girl in the picture on the next page doesn't live near any streams. To get water, people dug a well deep into the ground. A well is a tool for getting water, too. But it is not a simple tool like a bucket. How long do you think it took to make the well? Did one person make it, or more than one? What other tools do people need to make a well?

Where does the water come from in the last picture? What kind of tools did it take to make the sink?

Which is the easiest way to get water?

How else do people use tools? What tools can you name that help you get food? What tools help people make houses?

Human beings could not live without tools. Tools are part of human culture. People use tools for almost everything they do. One of the most important parts of growing up is learning to use new tools. What are the first tools a baby learns

to use? What tools can you use? What tools do you think you will learn to use?

Human beings can do more things with their hands than other animals. Humans also stand and walk differently from other animals. How do these differences make it easy for humans to use tools?

Using tools is an important part of being human. All human beings make tools. But not all people make the same kinds of tools. People used different tools to get water. Here are three different tools for sending messages. Which one do you know how to use? Which ones could you learn to use?

124

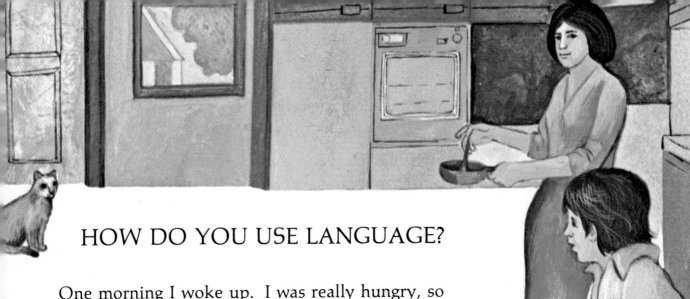

HOW DO YOU USE LANGUAGE?

One morning I woke up. I was really hungry, so I ran down to the kitchen.

"I'm hungry," I said to my mother. "What's for breakfast?" Mother gave me my breakfast.

"I want to go out and play," I told Mother. "May I?" Mother said yes and opened the door for me. I went outside.

Our cat came into the kitchen. "Meow," he said.

"You must want your breakfast, too," Mother said. She put some food in Cat's dish. Cat walked away.

"Meow," Cat said.

"Oh, you want to go outside," said Mother. She opened the door. Cat put out one paw. He sniffed the air. Then he backed away from the door.

"Meow."

"I wonder what Cat wants," Mother said.

How did Mother know what I wanted? Why didn't Mother know what Cat wanted?

Another part of human culture is **language** (LANG'gwij). Language lets you tell others what you are thinking. Not everyone speaks the same language, but all humans have a language.

People are not born knowing how to talk. Like other parts of human culture, languages are learned. When did you begin to learn your language? When you started school, did you learn a new language? Did you learn new things to do with your language?

Humans have found many ways to tell each other things. Language is more than words. Do you know what these people are telling you?

What do these things mean?

Suppose you were in another country where people spoke a different language. What problems would you have? How could you solve them? How would you let someone know you were hungry? Thirsty? Tired?

WHAT IS AN INSTITUTION?

How is Lynn's birthday different from Tula's? An animal grows older every year, just as a person does. But an animal does not have a birthday party, unless human beings give it one.

Lynn knows what will happen on her birthday. People will sing "Happy Birthday" to her. Probably her family will have a birthday cake for her. Perhaps she will get presents from some of her friends. How does Lynn know these things will happen? Will the same things probably happen on her birthday next year?

There are many things people do the same way, time after time. When your school has a fire drill, you know what to do. You know what the

Tula is eight years old today.

Lynn is eight years old today, too.

fire alarm means. You know how to line up and where to walk. Suppose a friend says to you, "We had a fire drill yesterday while you were at home sick." You don't need to ask, "What did everyone do?" You know what everyone did, because one fire drill is just like another.

A fire drill seems very different from a birthday party. But they are alike in one way. You know what will happen at each of them. Little things may change, but in most ways fire drills stay the same from year to year. So do birthday parties. So do holidays. So does school. Do you know what to expect when you start a new grade in the fall?

There is a name for all these things that we do the same way over and over. They are called **institutions** (in-stih-TOO'shunz). There are many different kinds of institutions. Holidays are institutions. You know what days they will be. You know what people will do to celebrate them, even though not everyone does exactly the same thing.

One reason that you know what to expect is that many institutions have rules. Fire drills have rules. What would happen if there were no rules for fire drills? Are there "rules" for what to do on holidays? Why do people often do the same things on a holiday every year?

Games are one kind of institution. Read the story on the next page. What happens when people don't know the rules for an institution?

The Crazy Game

Some friends invited David to play baseball with them. When David came to bat, the pitcher threw a football at him! David dodged it.

"Strike!" yelled the umpire.

"Strike? What do you mean?" cried David.

"You missed the ball," the umpire said.

"But that was a football."

"So what?" said the umpire. "A ball is a ball."

"Oh, all right," David said. "But how was I to know you were using a football to play baseball? Throw it."

This time David whacked the football. He ran to first base. But to his surprise, the first base player pushed him off the base. Then he tackled David to the ground and held him there until the pitcher came and tagged David with the football.

"You're out!" said the pitcher.

"You're crazy! This is the silliest game of baseball I've ever seen. I'm quitting," yelled David.

Why did David say the game was silly? What should the others have done, if they wanted David to play with them?

Institutions are part of human culture. That means all people have institutions. But not everyone has the same institutions. There are different institutions, just as there are different languages. There are different kinds of holidays. There are different kinds of schools. There are different kinds of games.

Look at these two pictures. Do you think these are institutions? Do you know what to expect when you go to these places? Do they have rules? What are the rules?

WHAT DO YOU BELIEVE?

Tools are part of human culture. Language is part of culture, too. So are institutions. But there is another part of human culture that you can't see or hear.

Beliefs are an important part of human culture. In fact, some people think beliefs are the *most* important part of culture. What people believe can change the way they live.

The two farms shown here may be only a few miles apart. But they are very different. The family on the first farm is Amish. They belong to a group of people who believe it is wrong to use modern machines. What differences can you find between the two farms? Can you think of other ways in which these two families are probably different? All these differences began because of different beliefs.

The Amish believe some machines are bad. It may be harder for you to decide what special beliefs the second family has. For many years, most Americans have shared a belief that machines are good. When many people have the same belief, it is often hard to understand that it *is* a belief. We just think that everyone agrees with our belief. Do the people on the second farm think machines are good? What do you think? Can machines be both good and bad?

People have beliefs about what is good and bad. They also have beliefs about what is true or false. For many years, some people believed that Earth was flat. Others believed it was round. How did they finally find out which was true?

People also have different beliefs about what is beautiful and what is not. Do you think this picture is beautiful? Do you know what it is? Does it matter what it is?

Do you ever disagree with others about what is beautiful?

You can see that beliefs change the way people live. Look at the list of beliefs below. Which of these beliefs do you agree with? Do you know anyone who disagrees with your beliefs? What do people who live in other places think? What did people in the past think?

It is wrong to eat any meat.
It is wrong to eat beef.
It is wrong to eat pork.
It is wrong to eat meat on certain days.
There is life in outer space.
There is life on Mars.
It is wrong to work on Sunday.
It is wrong to work on Saturday.
Walking under a ladder is bad luck.
Witches can make people sick.
The United States is the best place to live.
After I die, I will be born again as someone else.
After I die, I will live in another place.

Are some of these beliefs more important than others?

Here is a problem for you to think about. Mary is your *best* friend. One day Mary took John's pencil when he wasn't looking. You saw her take it. John asked Mary if she had his pencil. She said no. Then John asks you if you know where his pencil is. What will you say? How do you decide what is the right thing to do?

135

WHAT DOES CULTURE DO?

What is happening in each of these pictures? How is the girl's way of getting honey different from the bear's?

The big difference between the two pictures is human culture. Try to find the ways culture has helped the girl get the honey. Which way would you rather get honey? Why?

Is there any way the girl has used tools to get the honey? Is there any way she has used language? Language and tools are part of human culture.

Institutions are part of culture, too. Did any institutions help the girl get the honey?

138

Looking at Pictures

1. Look at the picture on page 120. List three ways this man can use language to find his way.
2. Look at the pictures at left. What parts of culture do they both show — tools, language, institutions, or beliefs?

What Do You Think?

3. Draw pictures of three different tools that are used for cooking.
4. Look at the picture at left. How do you believe these friends should act towards each other?
5. Suppose your school never has fire drills. What would you do if there was a fire? Why are institutions important?
6. Draw pictures of the different signs you see on your way to school every day.

1. Think of an animal that you've played with or seen. What needs do both you and that animal have?

2. Imagine you are a plant living on top of a mountain. Draw a picture of the kind of plant you would want to be. Remember: You have to protect yourself from cold, snowy winters.

3. Look at the picture of the squirrel. How are humans like squirrels?

4. Imagine yourself on a desert like the person in this picture. You have no food or water. What would you do? Who can live longer, you or the cactus plant? Why?

5. Culture is the human way of living. Think about the way you live. How is your way of life different from other animals? Write a poem about what you can do and other animals can't. Begin your poem with these lines: *I am a human being. I can . . .*

WHAT ARE GROUPS?

There are times when we like to be alone. But most of us like to be with other people. That is one of the things that makes us human.

We are members of many different groups. What are these groups? What does it mean to belong to them? Let's find out.

LIVING TOGETHER

These animals live together. They are called **social** (SOH'shul) **animals.**

AND LIVING ALONE

These animals live alone. They are called **nonso-cial animals.** What do *social* and *nonsocial* mean?

Tuma the Wolf

Tuma limped slowly and painfully along the slope. He had been hurt in a fight with a large deer. The wolf pack with whom he lived was five miles away. He would not be able to return to them.

Alone, tired, and in pain, Tuma came upon an empty cabin. He crawled in and lay down. As he drifted off to sleep, Tuma knew he might die in this old cabin. He was too badly hurt to hunt for food, so he might starve to death. He was also too weak to protect himself from other animals.

Feeling the warmth of the sun upon him, Tuma awoke the next morning. Unable to move, he lay and listened to the sounds of the forest. He thought of all the happy times spent with his pack. Tuma felt so alone. He wondered if he would ever see his pack again.

As darkness fell, Tuma's hunger grew. He tried again to get up, but it hurt too much. There was no way he could help himself.

Suddenly he heard the sounds of an animal

coming toward the cabin. His heart beat very fast. Fear raised the hair of his back. In the doorway stood a large black wolf. It was Denga, the strongest wolf in his pack and Tuma's closest friend.

Denga slipped into the cabin and dropped a piece of meat before Tuma. Then Denga left quietly.

Every night, one of Tuma's pack came to the cabin with a piece of meat for Tuma. Soon he was strong and well.

As he moved along the slope, Tuma felt happy. In just a little while he would be back with his pack once more.

You have learned that:

- Nonsocial animals live alone.
- Social animals live with others.

You live with others. You are social. All human beings are social.

Have you ever needed help from others? Write a story about what happened to you and how others helped you. Read your story to the class.

WHAT IS A GROUP?

In the last lesson you learned that humans are social. Humans are social because they live in **groups.** What is a group? Sometimes people in the same place and near each other are a group.

Sometimes people in the same place and near
each other are *not* a group.

What makes two or more persons a group?

Do these people *need* each other?   Are these people acting together?

Do these people have the same goal?

What do you think makes a group?

Some of the pictures on these two pages show groups. Some of the pictures *do not* show groups. Find the pictures that do show groups and tell the reasons for your choices.

Now look at the pictures that do *not* show groups. Explain why the people in these pictures are not groups.

You have found that a group is two or more
people

- who need each other,
- who speak or act together,
- who do something or enjoy something together.

Think of a group to which you belong. Tell
why you think it *is* a group.

THE GROUPS IN YOUR LIFE

Human beings are social. Many of the things they do are done with others.

Many things people do are done in groups. Everyone belongs to many groups. Look at the pictures on this page. They show Mary in some of the groups she belongs to. What would be a good name for each group? What are some of the groups you belong to?

WHAT TO DO?

My team expects
that I should be
at baseball practice
on Sunday at three.

My mother said
on Sunday at three
Aunt Betsy from Tulsa
is coming to tea.

I know my family is
counting on me
to see Aunt Betsy
who's coming at three.

I know my team is
counting on me
to pitch at practice
on Sunday at three.

Sometimes
I don't know
when to leave and
where to go.

Tell about a time when you felt
like the person in the poem.

COOPERATION AND CONFLICT

Sometimes members of a group **cooperate** (koh-OP'uh-rayt). You cooperate when:

You do your chores at home.

You wait your turn in line.

You agree to care for your little sister when your mother has work to do.

You play first base rather than outfield when the first baseman is absent.

You agree to see a movie rather than go to the museum because your friends want to see the movie.

There are many more ways in which you co-operate when you are in groups. Tell your class about one way in which you have cooperated with other people in a group.

Sometimes members of a group **conflict.** You conflict with others in a group when:

You and the other members of your family want to watch different TV programs at the same time.

You want the family to go on a picnic and your brother wants to go bowling.

You want to play ball, but your friends want to play a game of cards.

No one in your art class wants to pick up papers after an art project.

How else have you conflicted with a group to which you belong?

How have others in your group conflicted with the members?

Tell what you think *conflict* means.

The story below has no ending. You will make up two endings. Make up one ending that shows how members in a group can cooperate. Make up an ending that shows how members in a group can conflict.

Juanita and José are eating breakfast. Mother says: "You both have chores to do today. You are to fold the laundry, and separate it for each person in the family and put it on their beds. And one of you must also walk the dog."

"But Mother," Juanita says, "I can't do the chores. I'm supposed to go to the movies with my friend Ling."

"Well, I can't do them either," says José. "Carlos and I have made plans to go to the park and play ball."

Mother says: "Your plans are important, but the chores must be done."

Which of the pictures on the next page show conflict?

Which of them show cooperation?

Looking at Pictures

1. At left is a picture of some bees. Are bees social or non-social animals? Why?

2. Look at the picture of the Boy Scouts on page 149. What makes these boys a group?

3. The picture below shows a *group* of people. How are the people cooperating?

What Do You Think?

4. You learned in the story "Tuma the Wolf" that wolves are social animals. Pretend that Tuma *isn't* a social animal. How do you think the story would end?

5. Draw a picture of a group you belong to. In your picture show the reason it is a group. On the top of your drawing write the name of the group.

6. Why do you think humans like to live in groups?

WHAT IS YOUR COMMUNITY?

Here is another group to which people belong.
You and your family belong to it, too. What is
a good name for this kind of group?

159

You belong to a **community** (kuh-MYOO'nih-tee). On page 160 are some people who make up a community. What other people would you add to these?

You and your family depend on other people in the community.

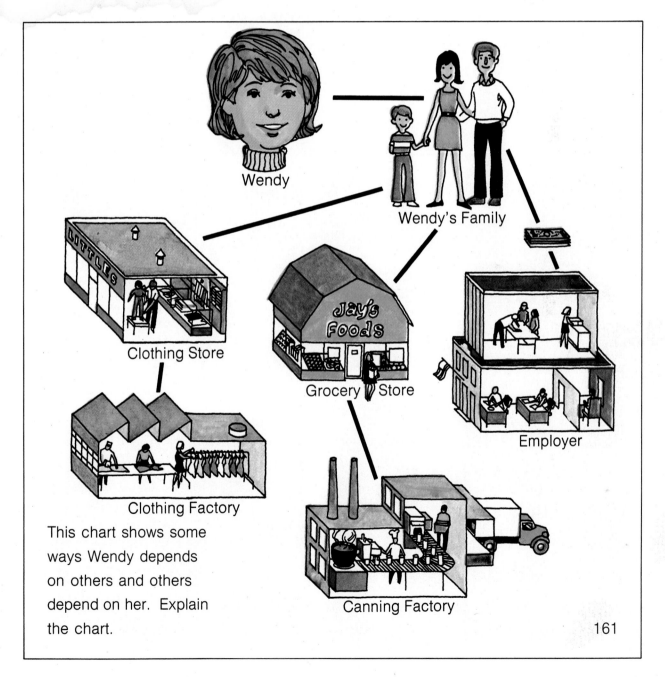

Wendy

Wendy's Family

Clothing Store

Grocery Store

Employer

Clothing Factory

Canning Factory

This chart shows some ways Wendy depends on others and others depend on her. Explain the chart.

161

A NETWORK OF PEOPLE

In a community, people who depend on one another form a **network.** What is a network?

A chain is a network, because each link depends on the next one. The chain is broken when one link breaks. A spider web is another kind of network.

Streets that cross each other also form a network. When you play a game of tag, you and your playmates also form a network.

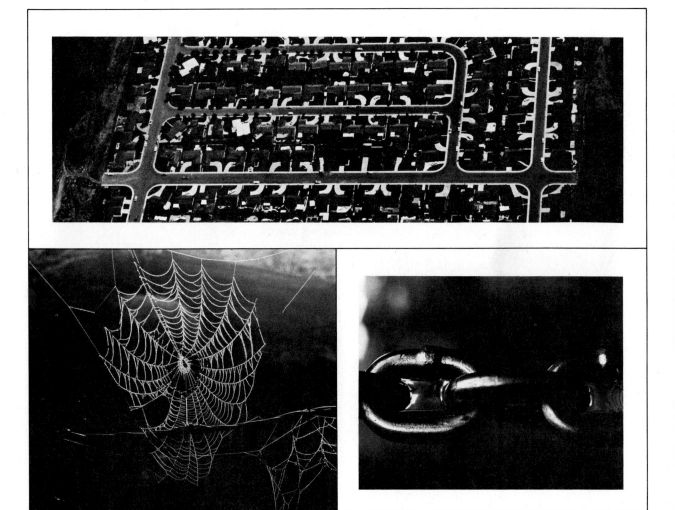

Family

Grocery Store

Meat Wholesaler

Trucking Company

Gas Station

Oil Delivery Service

Oil Refinery

Explain why the people in this chart form a network. Can you think of any other kinds of networks?

SHARING IN A COMMUNITY

People in a community share many things. Which pictures on this page show things that are often shared in a community?

What kinds of things that communities share
do these pictures show? Add some that you can
think of.   165

What is shared by communities in these pictures?

The Battle of Allatoona

The head of Georgia's Highway Department called the meeting to order.

"Ladies and gentlemen, we're here to discuss the route the new highway will take. I'd like to hear from our engineers. Would you explain this plan you've made?" he asked, pointing to the map.

Ms. Simpson answered first. "As you can see, the highway has already been built both from the North and the South. The last twelve miles will be connected at Atlanta. We must come to a decision soon about where the road is to be built."

Mr. Wilkes added, "The shortest way to connect the highway is to build a road through the parklands and over Lake Allatoona."

"Since that is the shortest way, it would take less time to build. Of course, it would also cost much less for two reasons. First, because it's shorter. Second, because the land belongs to the United States government and wouldn't cost us anything," said Ms. French with satisfaction.

Mr. Baskin then said, "All we will have to do is to build five big bridges across the lake."

The group agreed that this was the best way to connect the highway. They were sure they would receive permission from the United States government to go ahead with their plan. The meeting ended with all feeling very pleased.

SAILING ON THE LAKE

It was a warm spring day in 1970. Mr. Greear and his son were sailing their homemade sailboat on Lake Allatoona. The water sparkled like jewels.

Mr. Greear looked around him as the boat sailed smoothly through the water. He looked at the clear waters of the lake. As far as he could see there were tall, full trees surrounding the lake. He listened to the gentle sounds of the breeze and the birds. Mr. Greear felt this must surely be one of Earth's most beautiful places.

It was hard to believe that the crowded, busy city of Atlanta was only an hour's drive away. For

years people had come to Allatoona from far away to rest from city life and to enjoy nature.

Just about then, the sailboat arrived at the very spot where the huge concrete bridge was to be built. Mr. Greear had heard that five six-lane bridges were to cross the lake as part of a super-highway. He imagined how this natural beauty would be destroyed. He grew very angry. At that moment, he made a decision. He must stop the building of the highway over beautiful Lake Allatoona!

THE BATTLE IS ON

Mr. Greear studied the land around the lake. He talked about it with some engineers. (*Engineers* are people who know how to plan and to build things.) They found that it would save time and money to build the highway two miles to the west. Building it there would save the beauty of Lake Allatoona. It would also make the whole area around the lake look better.

Mr. Greear then went to the heads of the Georgia Highway Department. But they refused to change their plans. They said that Mr. Greear's plan would cost more and take longer. Some groups in the community agreed with the Highway Department and were against Mr. Greear's idea of building a highway west of the lake.

Mr. Greear then started to speak to other groups in the community. He spoke to

- families with summer homes in the area,
- Girl Scouts whose camps were in the woods around the lake,
- students
- a group of Navy people
- wildlife groups

When these groups heard Mr. Greear, they wanted to do something. This is what they did.

High school students set up tables on busy Atlanta streets so shoppers could write letters to Washington, D.C.

The Girl Scout Council wrote letters saying that their camps would be destroyed.

Wildlife groups all over the nation spoke of the danger to the birds and animals in the area. They too wrote letters.

A group of people from the Navy did a study. The study showed that the Highway Department plans were full of mistakes.

Thousands of people in Atlanta wrote letters to the White House and to the United States government. But the Georgia Highway Department

said: "No! No change in our plans!" Their engineers argued that the Greear plan would take four
years longer to build and would cost *14 million
dollars more!*

What is meant by "The Battle of Allatoona"?
Tell which groups you think were right and
why.

THE OUTCOME

Then, as the community battle was raging, something happened that affected the future of Lake
Allatoona.

The Supreme Court of the United States
ruled that the law protected public park land.
The Court said that such land could be used for
highways *only if no other route could be found.*

About the same time, the governor of Georgia ordered a new study comparing the Lake Allatoona route and the Greear route. The new study showed that the Greear route was better than the Highway Department's route.

The Georgia Highway Department engineers then said that they had been wrong. Instead of costing 14 million dollars *more*, the Greear route would cost 11 million dollars *less*. The Greear plan cost less because there would be fewer bridges.

On March 2, 1972, the governor of Georgia ordered the highway to be built around the lake.

Lake Allatoona, with all its natural beauty, has been saved.

Explain what the story, "The Battle of Allatoona," tells you about people in a community.

Looking at Pictures

1. A community is a large group of people. Look at the picture on page 159. How do people in a community depend on each other?

2. Turn to the picture on page 166. How might the people in this community feel if they didn't have a subway system? What might they do?

3. Look at the picture on this page. What does it show that most communities share?

What Do You Think?

4. Imagine that your community had a bad rain storm. Many of the streets and buildings are flooded. How might the people in your community cooperate to help those needing doctors, food, and clothing?

WHAT IS YOUR COUNTRY?

You belong to many groups.

Some of the groups you belong to are small, like your family and classroom.

Some of the groups are larger, like your community.

You also live in a still larger group.

This is the way this group looks on a map.

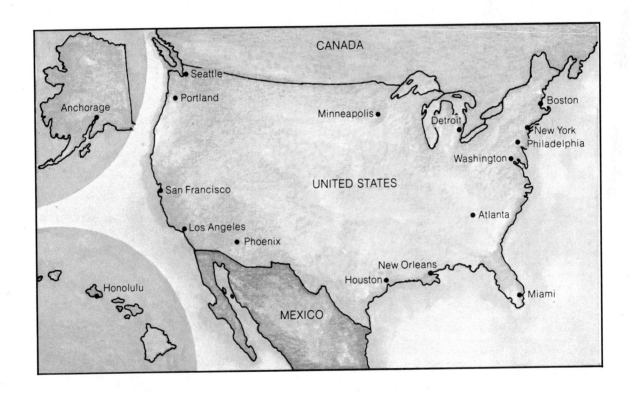

What is this group?

Why is the United States a group? It is a group because people who live in one part of the United States depend upon people who live in other parts of the United States.

The United States is also a **country.** What is a country? A country is a network of communities that depend on each other. Communities in a country depend on each other for **goods.** Goods are things humans make that people want or need. These pictures show how goods of one community reach other communities. Which of the communities do you depend on? Which depend on you? Explain.

ORANGES

The oranges in the picture above are from a California grove. The map at right shows where the oranges go after they are picked and put into crates.

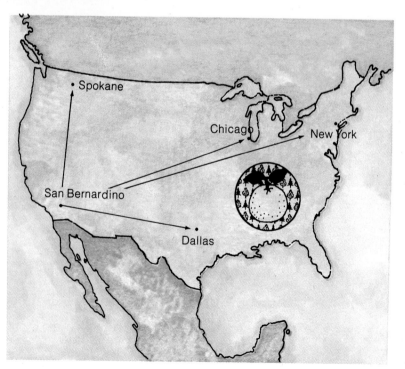

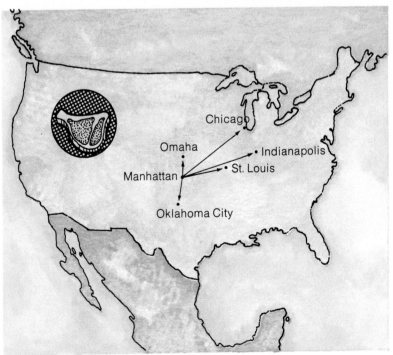

BEEF

The cattle grazing near Manhattan, Kansas, are sent to the places shown on the map. There they are killed and the meat is sold to stores all over the country.

177

CARS

The picture below shows a factory in Detroit where cars are made. The map at right tells where many of the cars from Detroit go.

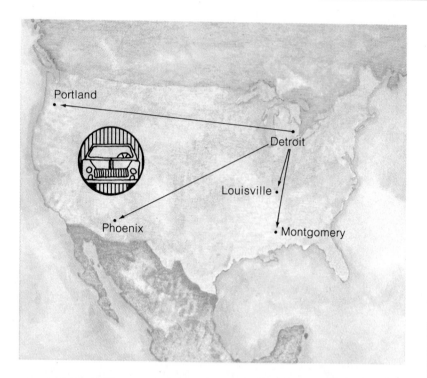

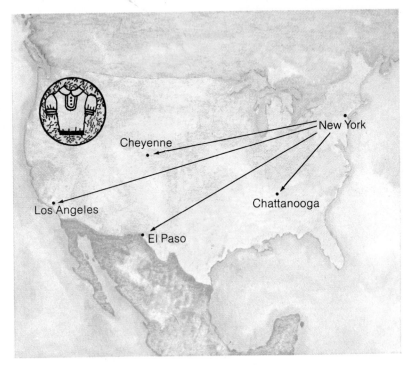

CLOTHES

The pictures above show clothes in a closet and clothes being made in a New York factory. The map at left shows where clothes are sent after they leave the factory.

179

Communities in a country need **services.** Services are kinds of work others do for us or we do for others. What services does your community have?

Communities don't have all of the services their people need. So communities depend on each other for some services. For example, all communities need teachers. But only some communities have schools for training teachers.

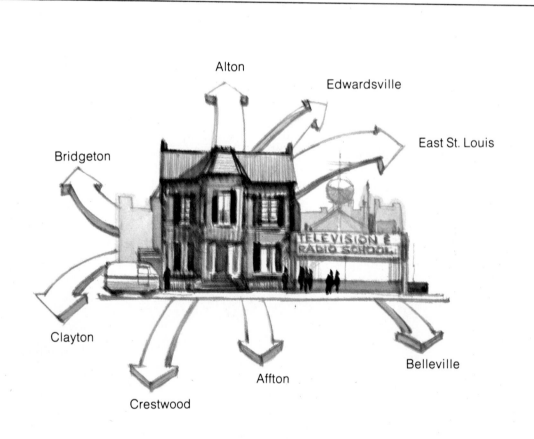

Alton

Edwardsville

East St. Louis

Bridgeton

TELEVISION & RADIO SCHOOL

Clayton

Crestwood

Affton

Belleville

How does the school in St. Louis provide services for people in other communities? Do other communities also provide services for St. Louis? What does this show?

WHAT DOES A COUNTRY SHARE?

What is a country? A country is *a network of communities that share some culture.* They share culture when they share institutions, tools, language, and beliefs.

SHARED INSTITUTIONS

Government is one institution that communities in a country share. The government of the United States gives services and makes laws, or rules, for all communities in the country. One of its services is the Postal Service.

The Story of a Letter

The picture at the right shows what happens when you mail a letter. Make up a story about the letter. In your story name the groups that helped in getting this letter to Santa Monica.

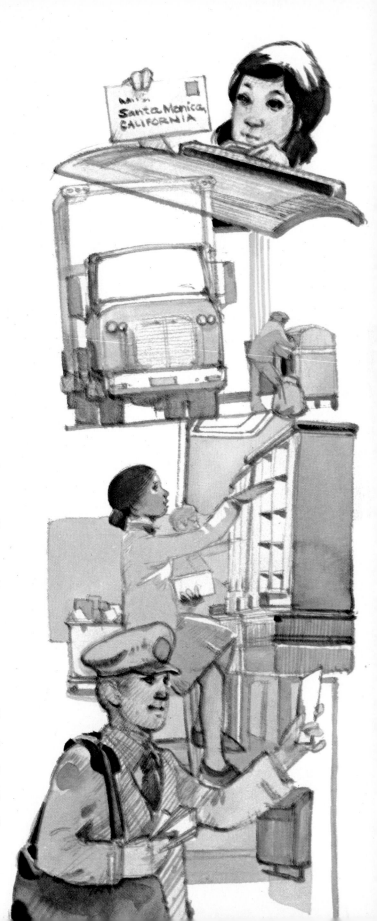

SHARED TOOLS

What does each of these networks make possible?

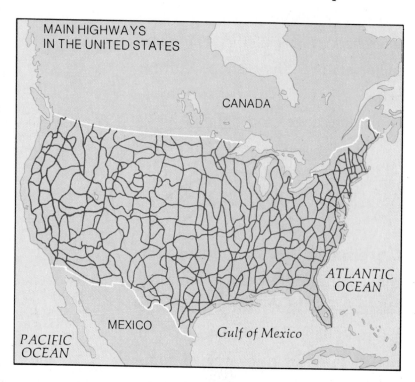

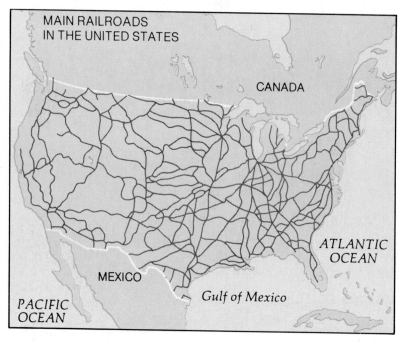

SHARED LANGUAGE

Many Americans have come from different countries. They often speak the language of the lands from which they came. What "languages" that all Americans understand do these pictures show?

A SHARED BELIEF IN FREEDOM

There are some beliefs which most people in the United States share. One of these is a belief that people should be free to do what they want as long as they don't hurt other people.

What freedoms are shown in these pictures? What other freedoms can you think of that are shared by people in the United States?

CONFLICT AND COOPERATION IN YOUR COUNTRY

What is a country? A country is *a network of communities that share some culture and sometimes conflict, sometimes cooperate.*

Communities sometimes conflict. Here is a case of conflict between people of two different communities. Read the newspaper stories below and see if you can tell how the conflict took place.

NEW HAMPSHIRE LOBSTERMEN ARRESTED OFF MAINE COAST

Concord, N.H. — Early yesterday, Maine police arrested two New Hampshire lobstermen who were fishing in "Maine waters."

The New Hampshire governor was told of the arrests. He then ordered New Hampshire police to arrest any Maine lobsterman found fishing in "New Hampshire waters."

The two states have never decided which areas of the ocean belong to each of them.

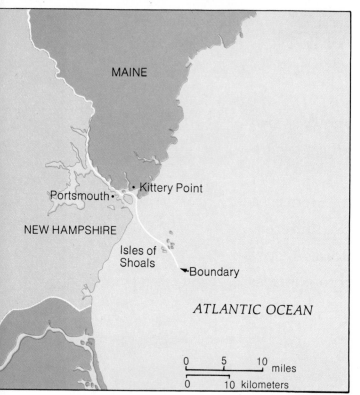

MAINE

• Kittery Point

Portsmouth •

NEW HAMPSHIRE

Isles of
Shoals

←Boundary

ATLANTIC OCEAN

0   5   10
└──┴──┘ miles
0   10 kilometers

WHERE THE
"LOBSTER WAR"
TOOK PLACE

In 1973 Maine police
arrested two New
Hampshire lobstermen
for fishing above the
line shown on this map.

LOBSTER CONFLICT CONTINUES

Talks between the governors of Maine and New Hampshire have failed to settle the conflict. New Hampshire people say that the lobster area they use has been theirs since 1940. Maine people say the lobster area they use has been theirs for over 60 years.

U.S. JUDGES TRY TO COOL MAINE-NEW HAMPSHIRE LOBSTER WAR

Two U.S. court judges have agreed to listen to both sides of the lobster conflict between New Hampshire and Maine. It is hoped that the judges will help to end the lobster war. Meanwhile the judges have ordered all arrests of lobstermen to be stopped.

How would you settle the conflict?

Communities sometimes cooperate.

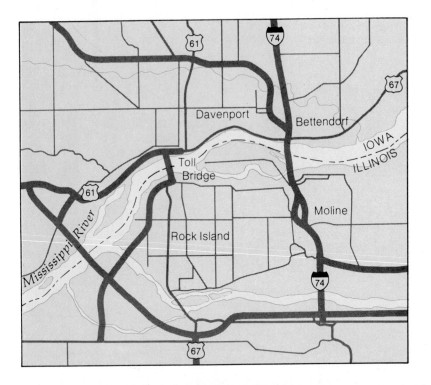

The communities of Rock Island, Illinois, and Davenport, Iowa, are shown on the map at left. They shared the cost of building the toll bridge shown below and help to take care of it.

187

The communities of New York and Newark cooperate in bad weather. When New York airports are foggy, and the Newark airport is clear, planes may land in Newark.

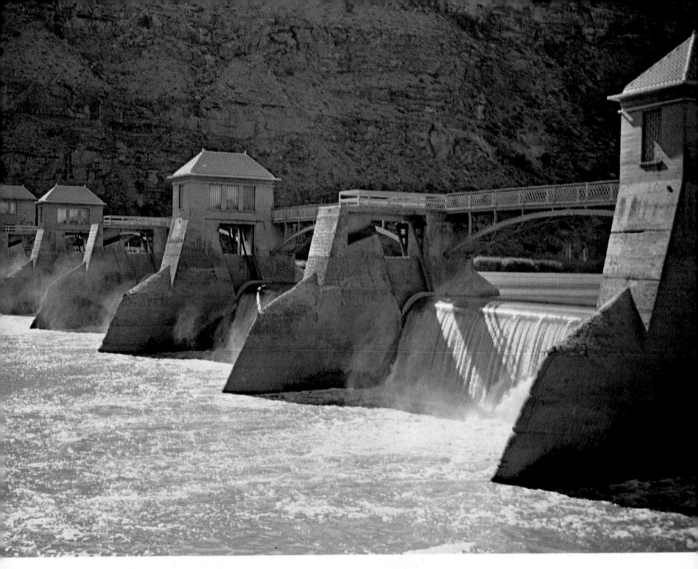

Why is cooperation needed here?

Find a story in your community newspaper that shows how your community cooperates with other communities. Explain how and why they cooperate. Find the communities on a map.

Find a story that shows a conflict between your community and one or more nearby communities. What started the conflict? What reasons does each community give for its side of the conflict?

189

Looking at Pictures

1. Look at the pictures on this page. List under the word "goods" those things in the pictures that are goods. List under the word "services" those things that are services.

2. A country is a network of communities. These communities depend on each other for goods and services.

Look at the map on page 179. Name a good that El Paso, Chattanooga, Cheyenne, and Los Angeles get from New York. What services are needed to get it there?

3. What part of culture do the pictures on page 182 show? How do communities in a country share this part of culture?

What Do You Think?

4. You learned that communities in a country share services. Boston is a community in the United States. It has a special hospital that can take care of children who are very badly burned. What service might Boston share with other communities?

5. Try to find out if the people of your community share something with the people in another community. They might share the same water supply or schools.

YOUR GLOBAL COMMUNITY

You belong to many groups.

You are a member of a family.

You are a member of a class.

You are a member of a community.

You are also a member of a country.

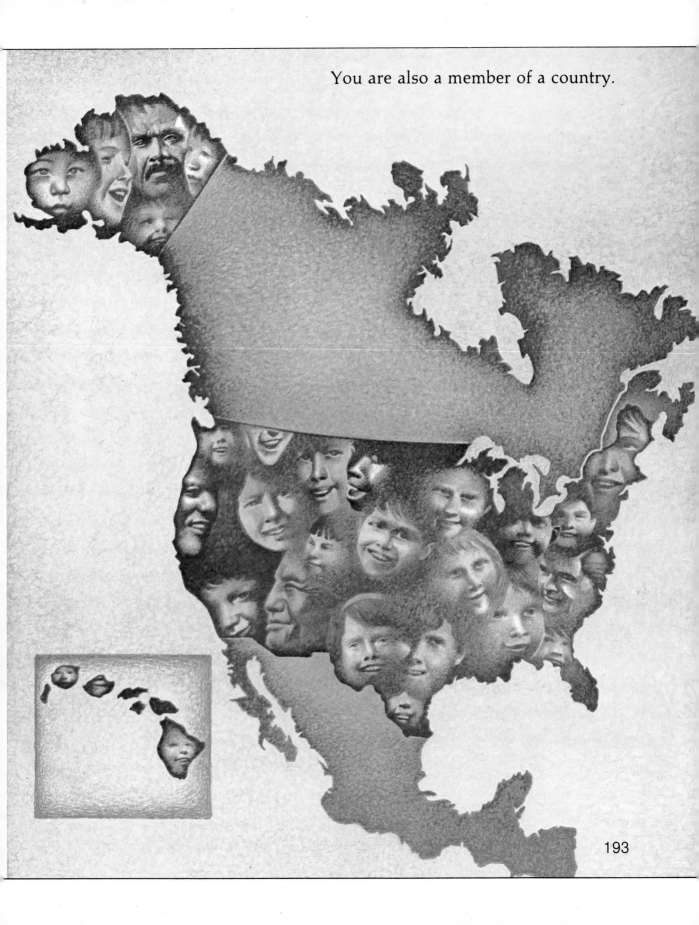

The largest group you belong to is the **global community.**

INTERDEPENDENT NETWORKS

The countries of the global community depend on each other. We say they are **interdependent** (in-ter-dee-PEN'dent).

Many countries form **interdependent networks.** Can you tell from this map why they do?

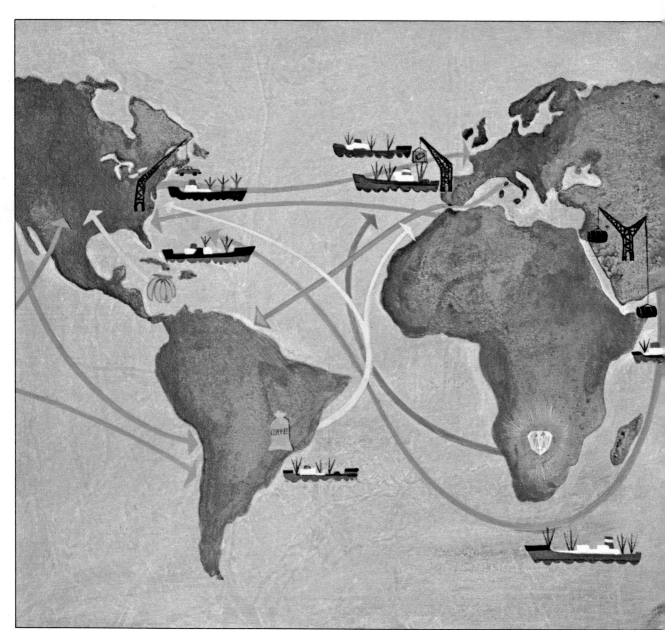

GOODS TRADED BETWEEN THE UNITED STATES AND OTHER COUNTRIES

This chart shows some of the goods we get from other countries and other countries get from us. Can you think of any other goods to add?

UNITED STATES   OTHER COUNTRIES

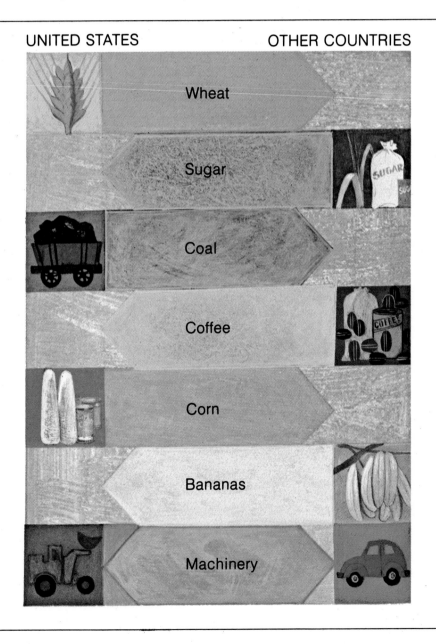

Wheat

Sugar

Coal

Coffee

Corn

Bananas

Machinery

Which goods from other countries does the United States depend on? Which goods from the United States do other countries depend on? What does this chart tell us about the global community?

197

WHAT DOES THE GLOBAL COMMUNITY SHARE?

SHARED INSTITUTIONS

People throughout the global community share some culture.

You share some culture with children in other countries.

Have you ever collected pennies for UNICEF on Halloween?

Classrooms for children

Health care for babies in Africa and Asia

Grain for hungry people around the world

Your pennies are added to those collected by children all over the world. The pennies are then sent to UNICEF.

Here are some of the things your pennies have helped to do for children in other parts of the world.

How do UNICEF activities show what is meant by a *global community*?

SHARED TOOLS

You share tools with persons in many parts of the world.

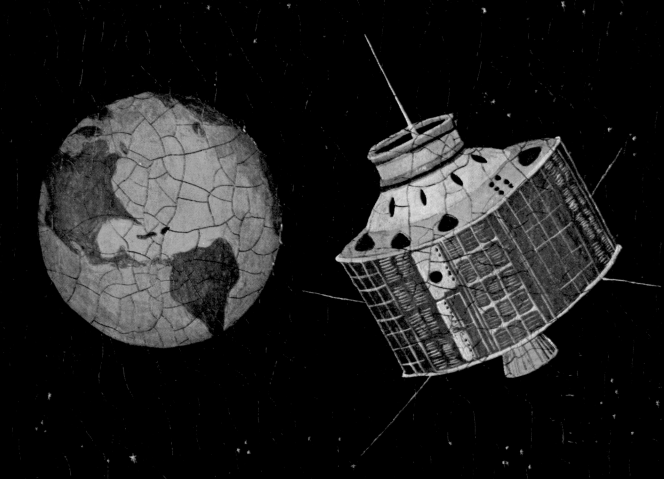

Satellites high above Earth bring TV programs and weather reports to people in many countries.

SHARED LANGUAGE

International Highway Signs

Signals at sea

These pictures show some of the forms of language shared by many countries of the world.

SHARED BELIEFS

All countries have ideas of fairness and justice. One idea of fairness is to settle a conflict by having two people fight it out. Another idea of fairness is to have a **court** settle the conflict. Here is a picture of a court. The judge listens to both sides and tries to decide fairly who is right.

Children's Rights

Another belief shared by many countries is the importance of children.

The United Nations drew up the Declaration of Children's Rights. These are the rights:

1. The child shall enjoy the rights stated in this Declaration.
2. The child shall enjoy special protection by law.
3. The child has a right to have a name and to be a member of a country.
4. The child has the right to grow and be healthy. The child has the right to good food, housing, and health services.
5. The child who is crippled shall be given special treatment and care.
6. The child needs love and understanding.

7. The child has the right to go to school. The child shall have exercise, fun, and play.
8. The child shall be among the first to receive protection and help.
9. The child shall not be hired for work until of proper age.

I am a child.
There are millions of children in
   the world.
The world belongs to children in
   a special way.
Because there are children, we
   know that the communities
   and countries of the world
   will continue in the future.

I am a child.
The world belongs to me in a special way.
Because of me,
   the world will go on.

Which of the children's rights is most important to you?

What right of children would you add to those of the United Nations' Declaration?

CONFLICT AND COOPERATION AMONG COUNTRIES

You have learned that you are a member of a country and that your country is a member of the global community. Members of the global community sometimes cooperate and sometimes conflict.

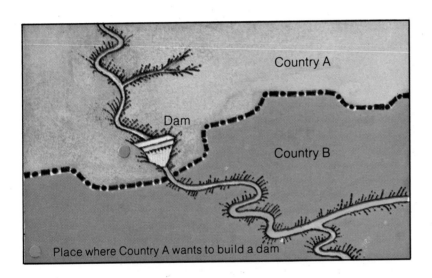

Place where Country A wants to build a dam

Why do countries conflict? Sometimes because there is not enough of what they need. Here is an example. A large river flows through two countries, Country A and Country B. The people of both countries need the water for drinking and growing food. But Country A wants to build a dam. This would hold back the water for Country B. The two countries conflict over what to do. They may meet together and work out a settlement. Or they may ask a third country, or the

United Nations, to help them. Perhaps both countries can work out and settle their conflict. Then we say they have ended their conflict peacefully.

But sometimes countries cannot settle their conflicts peacefully. Then they may try to use force. For example, they may stop trading with each other.

The worst kind of force countries use to settle

Many countries helped Florence, Italy, after a bad flood.

conflict is **war.** War is the worst way to settle conflict because it destroys life and property. For a country to take part in a war, it must spend much of its time and money in making guns, planes, and tanks. Its men and women must serve long periods of time in the army and navy. Even preparing for war uses up much of a country's time, money, and energy. That is why most countries do not want to go to war.

Many countries have given food to India in hard times.

COOPERATION

Countries also cooperate. They may cooperate with each other when something is scarce. These pictures show some examples of how countries may cooperate in difficult times.

207

Looking at Pictures

1. Countries in the global community are *interdependent.* What is one way the United States and other countries are interdependent? Look at the chart on page 197 to find out.

2. How does this panda show cooperation between countries?

3. The global community shares language. The two people in the picture below are from different countries. How are they talking? What are they saying?

What Do You Think?

4. Read again the Declaration of Children's Rights on page 203. Choose three rights that you believe. Do you think children in another country might also believe in them? Why?

5. What does "global" mean?

1. What do the people in your class do together? How do you and your class need each other? Why is your class a group?

2. Write a story about a conflict you once had with someone. What was the conflict about? How did you end the conflict?

3. List some services in your community.

4. This picture shows smoke from one community traveling to another community. What conflict might this smoke cause between these two communities?

5. Kim lives in Hawaii. He can talk to his friend Lenny in California. Look at the picture of them. What parts of culture does it show that people in the United States share?

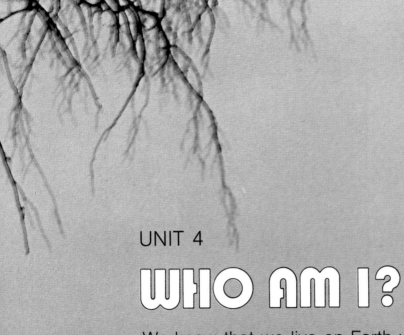

UNIT 4

WHO AM I?

We know that we live on Earth with many other living things. We know, too, that we are members of many different groups. But we need to know more. Even though we share many things with other people, each of us is a person. Each of us is *unique*. What does this mean?

211

HOW AM I LIKE ALL OTHER HUMAN BEINGS?

Look at the children in the pictures.
What is happening in each picture?
Do you know why?
Do ALL people do these things? Why?

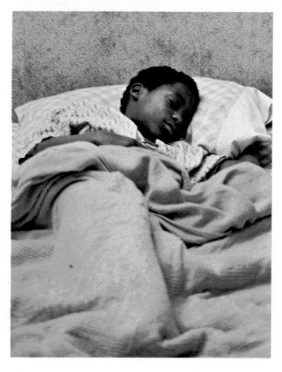

THE NEED FOR FOOD

I am like all other human beings because . . .
    I need food.

I eat.
I eat many different things.
I like to eat.

Why do I eat?
Why do I eat the things I do?
Why do I like to eat?

All of you from time to time have said, "I am hungry. I want something to eat." But are you really hungry? Do you really know what it feels like to be hungry?

213

WHEN I AM HUNGRY

When I am hungry,
I do not play.
I am not gay.
My world is gray,
When I am hungry.

When I am hungry,
I sing no song.
My day is long.
All things go wrong,
When I am hungry.

When I am hungry,
I think of food.
I remember food.
I dream of food.
I WANT food.
I NEED food,
When I am hungry.

Write a poem like the one you just read. Use the title "When I Am Tired" or "When I Am Cold."

214

THE NEED FOR SAFETY

I am like all other human beings because . . .

I need to *be* safe.

I need to *feel* safe.

What things in these pictures make us safe? Tell of some other things that make us safe. I also like to *feel* safe. But there are some things that frighten me. Some things frighten me more than other things.

The Giant Wave

I ran on the warm beach and I swam in the gentle surf. Suddenly I heard a roar. My heart beat wildly, for it was a sound I had heard before. I was so afraid! Suddenly I turned my head. And there he was — the giant wave!

He rocked back and forth. He swayed, hissed, and threatened me. I couldn't move. Then he curled himself into a huge arch. A mountain of water rose to the sky.

"Get away from me!" I cried.

"This time I've got you!" roared the wave.

He came at me.

"Help! *Help!* HELP!" I screamed.

"Chris, Chris, wake up." It was mother. She put her arms around me gently. "Nothing is going to hurt you," she said. I felt safe.

What was happening to Chris in the story?

Why was Chris frightened?

When did Chris feel safe? Why?

BEING ALONE

My mother has a job, so I have to let myself into our house every day after school.

I'm afraid to be alone. When I am inside, I lock the door. I'm so glad when my mother gets home! I talk to her while we fix dinner. She tells me how brave I am and how proud she is of me for staying alone until she gets home from work. Then I forget about being alone until the next day.

What is the person afraid of in the story?
Have you ever had this feeling?
Write down, or draw, the things that frighten you most. Tell how you are able to overcome your fear.

THE NEED TO LOVE AND BE LOVED

I am like all other human beings because . . .
 I need to love. I need to be loved.

 I have a puppy.
 He is black.
 My puppy has large brown eyes and silky
  fur.
 He is soft and plump.
 I cuddle him close to me.
 He feels warm.
 He always licks me on my face and nose.
 Sometimes I kiss him.
 I love my puppy.
 My puppy loves me.

Do you have a pet you love?
Name some people you love.
Why do you love them?

VALENTINE'S DAY

On Valentine's Day I got a stack of Valentine cards. They were fun to read and to look at. All but one. It had no name on it. There was an ugly face drawn on it. "THIS IS YOU," it said. Oh, did I get mad! Imagine someone sending me a card like that! And on VALENTINE'S DAY, too!

How would you feel if you got a Valentine like this? Why do you think someone sent the Valentine? How do you feel when you think someone doesn't like you?

CLASS PARTY

On the last day of school my teacher gave a class party. At first I just looked on. I didn't know what to do or how to act. I was afraid. Then everyone made a circle around me. "Come on, join the fun," they said.

We played games. Every time I won I'd laugh loudly and clap my hands. I sang when the music played my favorite song. Then we all sang together. Sometimes we giggled and moved around the room and did silly things. The more I could join in with the others in the class, the happier I became.

Why did the person in the story become happy? Would the person act the same way alone? Why?

THE NEED TO BELIEVE IN YOURSELF

I am like all other human beings because . . .
I need self-respect.
I need to be able to do some things.
I need to believe I can do some things.
I need to believe in myself.

I had always wanted a two-wheel bicycle. I dreamed of riding it to school, waving to my friends. I dreamed I was the best bike rider in my neighborhood. In my dream, all the kids said, "Gee, you're *good!* We wish we could ride as well as you do!"

On my eighth birthday my dream came true. I got a two-wheeler as a present. I was so excited, I rushed outside to try it. Now was the time for me to show everyone what I could do. I jumped onto my bike. But it flipped me over to the ground. I tried again and again, but each time I took a spill. I was making a fool of myself. I felt like crying. What was wrong? Why couldn't I ride my new bike? After a while I gave up and sat on the curb trying to hold back the tears.

My older brother saw what was happening.
When he saw I wasn't trying any more he said,
"Come on, try again." But I was so discouraged
and ashamed I just wanted to run away and hide
so I could cry where no one would see me.

"No," I said, shaking my head. "I don't
really like this bike. It's not what I wanted
anyway."

"Oh come on," my brother insisted.
"Learning to ride a bike takes practice.
Here — I'll help you. I'll hold you up
until you get the feel of the bike and
you can learn to peddle it. Then I'll
turn you loose and you can go on
your own. You can do it," he said.

After going
around the block
several times with
my brother holding
me up, I managed to
peddle and also
keep the bike from
toppling over.

Finally, he turned me loose. Although I wobbled at first, I was able to keep the bike from falling over, and I was peddling. I was not exactly the great bike rider I had dreamed of being, but I was holding my own. I felt good.

Have you ever wanted to do something very much and found you could not do it? How did you feel?

Have you ever learned to do something you wanted very much to do? How did you feel?

Do you feel that being able to do something you really want to do is important? Why?

Write a paragraph about the thing you would most like to be able to do.

THE NEED TO BE YOURSELF

I am like all other human beings because . . .
    I need to be myself and nobody else.

YOU AND I ARE FRIENDS

You and I are friends. One day we were talking
to each other. Here's how it went:

You: I like to swim. I love to feel the water on
        my body.

Me: I hate swimming. It makes me feel so
        WET! YUK! I love to go camping. I like

to run through the trees. And at night I
watch the stars come out.

You: CAMPING! How can anyone like camping All those bugs biting you. Sleeping on
the ground. No, camping is not for me.
Now, when you go swimming you can
play in the sand and listen to the waves.

Me: Why would anyone want to play in sand?
It gets into your ears, eyes, and onto your
food. Sand makes me scratch! Waves
make too much noise. The sound gives me
a headache! When you go camping it is
nice, quiet and cool.

You: *I like swimming!*

Me: *I like camping!*

You: YOU don't have to like what I like!

Me: I don't have to like what YOU like!

Both: But, YOU and I are *still* friends.

Have you ever had a friend that didn't like the
things you liked?

Were you able to get along with each other?

Do you think it is important to do what you like
to do?

How would you feel if you had to do just exactly
what everyone else was doing?

THE NEED TO KNOW

I am like all other human beings because . . .
I am curious about other places, people and things.

THE OTHER SIDE OF THE WALL

We had just moved to a new apartment. Behind the building was a big brick wall. Why had someone put such a big wall there? What could be on the other side? I wondered about the wall. Was it to keep me out or to keep something else in? The wall was much higher than I was, so I couldn't see over it. How could I find out?

After thinking about it for awhile, I decided to climb the wall. But it was too slippery. There was nothing to hold on to.

"Why not call to the people on the other side and ask, 'Who's

there?' " I thought. So in a big voice I yelled, "Is anybody over there?" But no one answered.

"I know what I'll do," I thought. "I'll pull a brick out of the wall and spy through the hole." I looked and found a brick that was loose. I tried, but I could not pull it out of the wall.

"Now what?" I sat down on the ground and thought. "I'll throw some pebbles over the wall. If there is anyone standing on the other side, they will be sure to yell out." I picked up three small pebbles and tossed them over. I waited for someone to say something. But there was not a sound.

"What's wrong? Why didn't somebody yell at me?" Suddenly a great idea came to me. Why not make a stairway and climb up? In the basement of our building, I found some moving crates. I took them outside in the yard near the wall, and arranged them carefully. After several hours of work, the last crate was set in place. And now for the big moment. My heart pounded, and I shook with a little fear. Should I risk climbing up and looking over the wall after what I had done? What if someone were standing there ready to scream at me?

Soon I made my decision. "Here goes," I whispered to myself in a small shaky voice. Carefully and quietly I mounted the crates. I stopped for a few seconds. I waited. Slowly I raised my head above the wall. I kept my eyes closed for a moment, waiting for the worst. Then I opened them. There it was — the other side of the wall.

What do you suppose was on the other side of the wall? Why was the person in the story so eager to find out? Would you have acted in the same way?

Have you ever been very, very curious about something? What did you do?

How do you feel when someone keeps a secret from you?

Are all people curious? What do people do when they are curious? Why are the people in these pictures doing what they are doing?

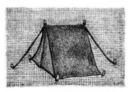

Looking at Pictures

1. Look at the pictures on page 212. What do these pictures show that all humans need?

2. The picture at left shows things that help humans feel safe. How do they all give a feeling of safety?

3. The pictures below show a need that humans have. Name the need.

4. Turn to the picture on page 224. What need is this boy meeting?

What Do You Think?

5. What is something you've been curious about? How did you find out about it?

6. All human beings need to believe that they can do some things. What do you believe you can do well?

I LOOK MORE LIKE SOME PEOPLE THAN OTHERS

People are all alike in many ways. People share many of the same needs. But people are not exactly alike — otherwise how could we tell one person from another? How are people different, and how are they alike?

I look more like some people in my class than others.

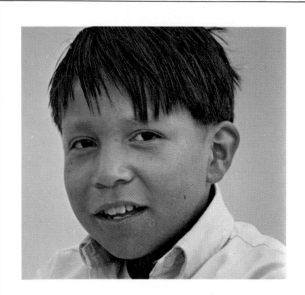

Look at the people in your classroom. Do you see anyone whose eyes are the same color as yours? Do you see anyone whose hair is the same color as yours? Do you see anyone whose skin is the same color as yours? Do you see anyone who is the same height you are?

Do you see anyone whose face is the same shape as yours? Do you see anyone who has the same shape lips as yours?

Do you see someone who has the same color of eyes, color of hair, height, face shape, shape of lips, *and* color of skin as you have?

Is there anyone in your classroom that looks *exactly* like you? Do you look more like some people than others?

233

A FAMILY CHART		Color of Hair	Color of Eyes	Ears	Lips	Shape of Face
Pedro		dark brown	black	medium	full	round
Pedro's Mother		brown	dark brown	small	full	oval
Pedro's Sister		black	light brown	medium	small	oval

Look at the chart above.

How is Pedro like his mother?

How is Pedro like his sister?

Were there things about Pedro more like his mother than like his sister?

Is Pedro *exactly* like his mother or his sister?

What does this chart tell you?

On another sheet of paper, make a chart like this one for yourself. Take the chart home. Find out about the faces of two other people in your family. Put the information into the chart. Then compare yourself with the other two people in your family. Whom do you look like?

I ACT MORE LIKE SOME PEOPLE THAN OTHERS

I belong to many groups. I share some culture with other members of these groups. I have learned many of the things I do in these groups. These are some of the groups I learn from.

Joan

I am Joan.
I live in the United States.
I speak English.
I play softball.
I wear a dress or jeans to school.
I like hamburgers.

Ahmed

I am Ahmed.
I live in Egypt.
I speak Arabic.
I like to play "Hunt the Fox."
I wear an aba (robe) to school.
I like to eat kibbe (meat loaf).

Masako

I am Masako.
I live in Japan.
I speak Japanese.
I like to play volleyball.
I wear a uniform to school.
I like to eat udon (noodles).

Nino

I am Nino.
I live in Italy.
I speak Italian.
I play soccer.
I wear short trousers to school.
I like to eat spaghetti.

237

On another sheet of paper, make a chart like this. Fill in the blank spaces with the right words.

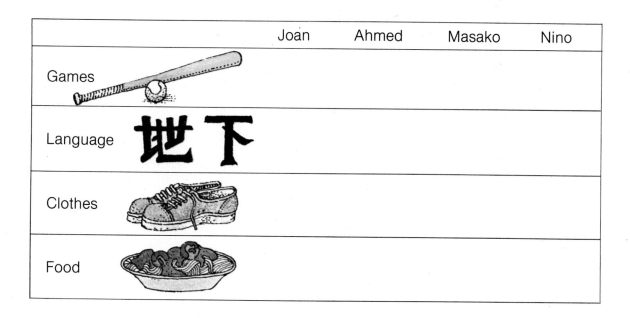

	Joan	Ahmed	Masako	Nino
Games				
Language				
Clothes				
Food				

If Joan had grown up in Italy, what language do you think she would speak? Would she be more likely to eat spaghetti or hamburgers?

If Ahmed had grown up in Japan, what game might he learn to play?

If Masako had grown up in the United States, what might she wear to school?

Suppose you had grown up in Egypt. What language would you speak? Do you think you might like to eat kibbe rather than your favorite food now?

Compare yourself with the other children in the chart. Which boy or girl are you more like? Tell why this is so.

SANFORD'S STORY

SANFORD   DAVID   YOUNG-MI   PABLO   JANE   CHERYL

My name is Sanford. I am in third grade. In my classroom I am in Group I. There are five other persons in my group. They are David, Jane, Young-Mi, Pablo, and Cheryl.

One day our teacher asked us to write a story on "How I Am More Like Some People Than Others." She told us to compare ourselves with other members in our group.

Here is my story:

I am Sanford.
In my group I am like David and Pablo.
They are boys, too.

I am short.
In this I look like Jane.
She is short, too.

I am brown.
In this I look like Young-Mi and Pablo.
They are brown, too.

I have black hair.
My black hair looks like Young-Mi's and Pablo's.
They have black hair, too.

I sing well.
In this I am like Cheryl.
She sings well, too.

I enjoy drawing.
In this I am like Young-Mi.
She enjoys drawing, too.

I enjoy eating hot dogs.
I am like the whole group.
We all enjoy eating hot dogs.

I can't run very fast.
I am like David and Jane.
They can't run fast, either.

I'm good in math and science.
I'm like Young-Mi and Pablo.
They are good in math and science, too.

I speak English.
I am like the whole group.
We all speak English.

I play softball.
I'm like Young-Mi, David, and Cheryl.
They play softball, too.

I am like my whole group.
We all enjoy school.

Sanford

P.S. I liked writing this story. I
found out that I am like different
kinds of people. This is good to
know.

Look at the pictures of Sanford and his
friends. How are you more like some of them
than others?

242

Looking at Pictures

1. Choose two faces from the pictures on page 232. How are these people alike? How are they different?

2. Look at the picture of the children playing instruments. Choose one child. How is that child acting more like some of the children in the picture than others?

3. How is the child in the bottom picture like you? How is she different?

What Do You Think?

4. Choose one of the children shown on page 236 or 237. Pretend that you are that person. Write a story about what you might do during a school day.

5. Choose a student in your class who is more like you than the other students. Tell why you are more like that person than others.

HOW AM I UNIQUE?

I am **unique** (yoo-NEEK'.)
I am one of a kind.
I am a combination of many things.
I am not exactly like anyone else.

What does it mean to be unique? Look at the greatly enlarged pictures of snowflakes. How are they different from each other? When it snows, there are millions of snowflakes in the air. But no two snowflakes are exactly alike!

243

Look at the seashells. Notice
how they are alike and how they
are different. Can you find any
that are exactly alike?

In a flower garden, can you
find two flowers that are exactly
alike in size, shape, color, and design?

244

These two zebras look alike at first. But look closely. Can you see any differences? Do you think any two animals are exactly alike?

Here is a pair of human twins. Can you see any differences between them? Do you know any twins? Do they look and act exactly the same?

I Am the Only Me in All the World

I am me.
I am like no other person.
There are things about me different from every other person.
I do not look like you.
My smile, voice, and fingerprints are different from yours.
I do not act the same way you do.
My feelings are special.
I have different talents and different skills from yours.
The things I make are not the same as the things you make.
I see things differently from the way you see them.
The things I want and need are not exactly the same things you want and need.

I am the only me in all the world.

"I am one of a kind." Does it mean there's never going to be another me in all the world, now or ever?

ME AND MY FEELINGS

Me on the Outside

What does the word *me* mean?
Me is —
   A photograph of myself
   When someone says my name
   Something I've made
   My voice played on a tape
      recorder
   My echo coming back to me
   My shadow
   A painting of me
   My name written
   My face I see in a mirror

Faces of Me

I really have many
faces.
Some of them I can
see in a mirror.
I see different kinds
of faces.
Sometimes I see a
happy face.
Sometimes I see a
sad face.
Some of my faces I
like, some I don't
like.
*But all the faces I see
in the mirror are
me.*

What else can you
think of that means
you? Make a "Me"
book. Write all the
things you think
means "you." Draw
pictures to go along
with your words.

249

Clowns

Clowns are funny. They make me laugh. I feel happy when I watch them. They have big noses and squizzly hair. Their mouths are large and wide. Some of their mouths turn up, some turn down. Clowns wear baggy pants and big, floppy shoes. They do funny tricks. Every time I see a clown, I laugh, and laugh and laugh.

What other things besides clowns make you laugh?

SOMETIMES I FEEL HAPPY

I am happy when I am treated nicely and when people like me. When I do something for others, that makes me happy too. I am also happy when people share with me and when they play fair. I am happy when someone says I have done something well. Being happy is a good feeling.

Do you feel good when you do something for someone else? Why?

SOMETIMES I AM SAD

A little gray squirrel used to play in the big oak tree outside my window. I loved to watch him scampering up and down the tree. He would leap high in the air and spring onto the branches. I really liked that squirrel!

But one day the squirrel did not come. He never returned. I felt very sad.

When I am sad, I am very quiet.
I don't feel like talking.
I sit alone in a big chair.
I do not watch TV.
I do not play.
I do not draw.
I do not eat.
I just sit quietly.
I feel so alone when I am sad.

What do you do when you are sad? How do you feel?

251

I WAS ANGRY

Once I got punished for something I did not do.
An awful feeling came over me. I tried to get rid
of the feeling by screaming and yelling and jumping up and down. The awful feeling did not go
away, so I ran to my bed and lay across it. I
banged my fists down on my bed several times.
I then cried as hard and loud as I could. My
hollering and yelling made my head hurt, and I
became very tired and sleepy. Soon I fell asleep.
When I woke up I felt better. The awful feeling
had gone away. I felt dull.

How would you have felt in this situation?
What would you do if you were punished for
something you did not do?

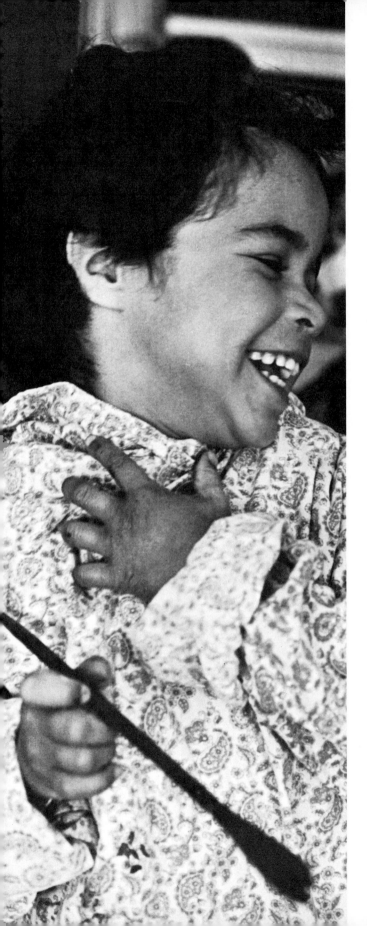

WHAT I DO WITH MY FEELINGS

I have many feelings. Everyone does. I do very different things according to the different feelings I have. If I am frightened, I act in a certain way. If I am sad, I act another way. I do not do the same thing when I am frightened as when I am sad. Nor do I do the same thing every time I am frightened, or every time I am sad.

Think of a time when you were happy. What made you happy and how did you show it? Describe a time when you were sad, frightened, and angry. What did you do each time? How do you think the child in this picture feels — sad, frightened, angry or happy? Why?

253

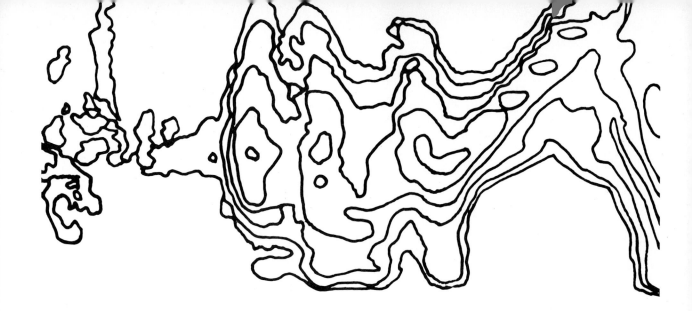

MAKING A CHART OF ME

Pictures of me show that I am not the same as everyone else. My fingerprints show this, too.

My voice is also different from everyone else's. Have you ever been able to tell who someone is just by listening to that person's voice? How many people do you know by their voices?

A **voice print** is a chart of the sound waves made by a person's voice. It is something like a fingerprint. It is different for each person. Here is a picture of a voice print.

The things we do can be made into a chart. On the next page is a chart showing some of the things I do. The chart shows how good I am at these things.

On a separate sheet of paper, make a chart like this one for yourself. Put an "X" on the line where it belongs to tell how well you do each thing. Then draw lines to connect the X's. Compare your chart with the charts made by your classmates.

MY CHART OF ME	Don't do	Do poorly	Do well	Do very well
Ball:				
throwing			X	
catching				X
batting		X		
Jumping rope:				
running in		X		
jumping			X	
running out		X		
Swimming:				
under water	X			
floating		X		
diving	X			
above water		X		
Bike riding:				
2-wheeler			X	
3-wheeler	X			
riding for a long time			X	
Building models:				
putting together		X		
painting				X
Art work:				
drawing with pencil			X	
watercolors	X			
crayons		X		
Music:				
singing				X
playing an instrument		X		
learning words		X		
My own thing:				

Looking at Pictures

1. Look at the picture on page 251. Why do you think this child is sad?

2. Compare the chart you made of yourself with the chart on page 255. Which things can both you and the child in the book do well?

3. Make a copy of your fingerprint. Compare it to this fingerprint. How is your fingerprint unique?

4. Is your handwriting exactly like any of those shown on this page?

What Do You Think?

5. List five things or people that make you happy. Write beside each the reason it makes you happy.

6. Do you think the same things make everyone angry? Why?

7. Draw a picture of someone who is angry.

1. List some of the needs which all humans have. Would these needs be the same if people lived in different places? Why?

2. Tell about a time when you felt lonely. What made you stop feeling lonely?

3. Carole is a third grader who is curious about turtles. She wants to find out how they live, what they eat, and how big they are. Name some different ways she might find these things out.

4. Look at the picture of the Japanese family eating. How is their way of eating like the way your family eats? How is it different?

5. Imagine that each of your classmates is *not unique.* They are all exactly like you. How might this change your class?

6. This picture shows greatly enlarged grains of sand. How is each grain unique?

Who Are We?

You are a human.
Where do humans live?

All humans need certain things to stay alive. How does Earth's life-support system help us to meet these needs?

Humans live together on Earth with many other living things. But humans are different because of their culture. What parts of culture does this picture show?

My dog and I went for a walk.

I saw a

My dog saw the

I said, "This is a flower."

Why didn't my dog say what I said?
He saw the same thing.

Next I saw a

My dog saw the

I said, "Go away, bee."
My dog just barked.

Why didn't my dog say what I said? Why didn't
I bark like my dog?

We went home.
I said to Father, "I saw a pretty flower with a bee
on it."
"What did you see?" Father asked my dog.
My dog barked.
Why didn't my dog tell Father what he saw? Will
he ever be able to tell what he saw?

Because humans are social animals, we often do things together. We belong to groups. Does this picture show a group? Give reasons for your answer.

Does this picture show cooperation or conflict? Give reasons for your answer.

One important group that you belong to is your community. How do the members of your community act towards each other? What do the members of your community share?

This picture shows part of one community. What do the people in this community share?

Another important group that you belong to is your country. People living in the same country share institutions. In the United States people share the holiday of July 4. This is the birthday of the United States. What else do members of a country share?

Countries all around the world cooperate with each other to plan the Olympic Games. Many different countries send their best athletes to play against each other.

Even though you belong to many different groups, you are always you. You are different from everyone else.

265

FINDING THE WAY

Mr. Winter thinks he is lost. Find the X on the map. The X marks the spot on Maple Street where Mr. Winter is standing. Find the symbol for Mr. Winter's home. Help him to use map language to find his way home. Use the **compass rose** to help you find *direction* (which way to walk). Write your answers on a separate sheet of paper.

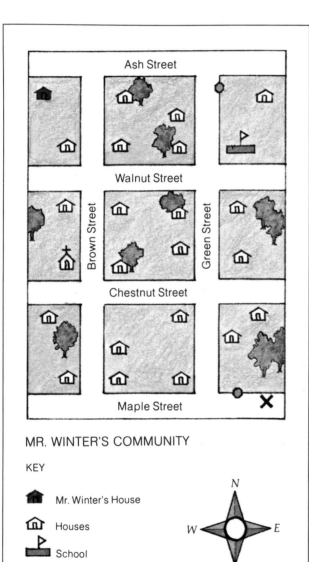

MR. WINTER'S COMMUNITY

KEY

Mr. Winter's House

Houses

School

Stop Sign

Church

Compass Rose

1. Mr. Winter should move _____ (east or west) to the stop sign.
2. Then he should turn right and walk along Green Street toward the _____ (north or south).
3. On Green St., he will pass a [symbol]. This symbol stands for a _____.
4. What will he see at the corner of Green and Ash Streets? Its symbol is ⦿ .
5. When he gets to Ash Street, he should turn left. Then he should walk toward the _____ (east or west).

ESTIMATING

Did anyone ever ask, "How high can you jump?"
Did you say, "About so high"?

When you answer in this way without counting or measuring, you are **estimating.** Estimate answers to these questions on a separate sheet of paper.

1. The top map shows two towns. The key shows that each dot equals 100 people. Which town has more people?

2. The bottom map shows three ways you can go from the school to the candy store. Use the map and estimate the shortest way from the school to the candy store. *Rule:* You have to stay on a street.

(Check your answers with those on page 276.)

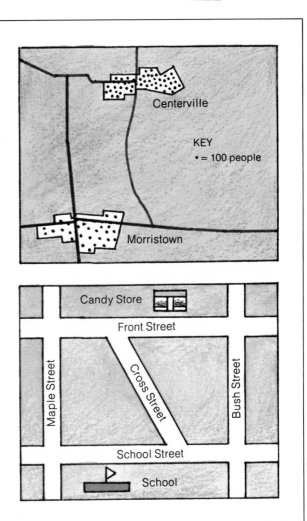

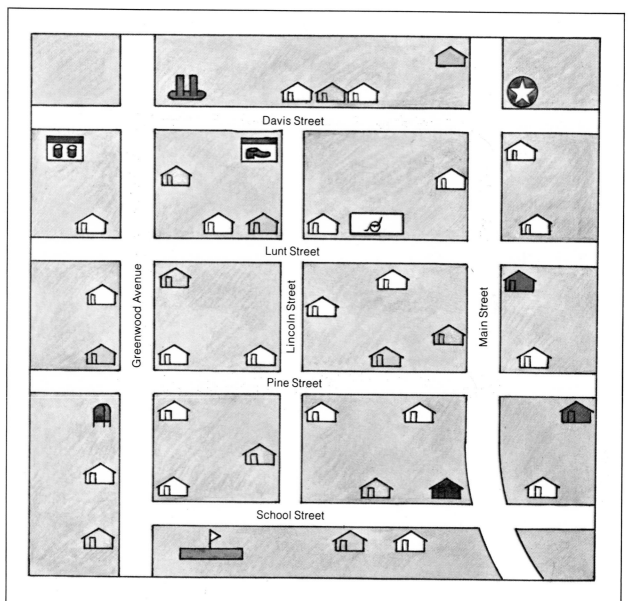

Davis Street

Greenwood Avenue

Lunt Street

Lincoln Street

Main Street

Pine Street

School Street

MAP OF A SMALL COMMUNITY

KEY

Mrs. Rodino's House

Bill's House

Paul's House

Hospital

Police Department

Post Office

Gas Station

School

Shoe Store

Grocery Store

N
W   E
S

GROUPS IN A SMALL COMMUNITY

You can use a map to find where groups are *located* (where they are found) in a community. Use the key to help you find the shoe store. The shoe store is located on Davis Street. If you walked along Davis Street, you could move toward the east or the west. Use a separate sheet of paper to write down answers to the questions below.

1. On what street do the teachers work?

2. On what street do the doctors and nurses work?

3. A mail carrier delivers mail from the Post Office to places on Greenwood Avenue. In what direction would the mail carrier walk to go from the Post Office to the gas station?

4. Mrs. Rodino is a policewoman. She lives on Main Street. She walks north to the police station every morning along Main Street. How many streets does she cross to get to work?

5. On what street is the grocery store?

6. In what direction would you walk to go from the shoe store to the grocery store?

7. Find Paul's house on Pine Street. Find Bill's house on Lunt Street. Who has to walk farther to school, Paul or Bill?

8. Whose family has to drive farther to the gas station, Paul's or Bill's?

(Check your answers with those on page 276.)

IN-BETWEEN DIRECTIONS

On page 271 is a map of Texas. Use a finger on your right hand to point to the city of Fort Worth. Move your finger from Fort Worth to Waco. You were moving *south*. Now move your finger back to Fort Worth. Then move from Fort Worth to Dallas. You were moving *east*.

Go back to Fort Worth. Keep your finger on Fort Worth. Find the city of Houston. Move your finger from Fort Worth toward Houston. You were moving toward the south *and* the east. Map-makers call this direction *southeast*.

Go back to Fort Worth. Point to Lubbock with your left hand. Move your right finger from Fort Worth toward Lubbock. You are moving north *and* west, or northwest.

A compass rose like the one shown on page 271 is used to show in-between directions.

Use the map of Texas and the compass rose to answer these questions. Write your answers on a separate sheet of paper.

1. In what direction would you move to go from Lubbock to Austin?
2. In what direction would you move to go from Austin to San Antonio?
3. In what direction would you move to go from Corpus Christi to San Antonio?

(Check your answers with those on page 276).

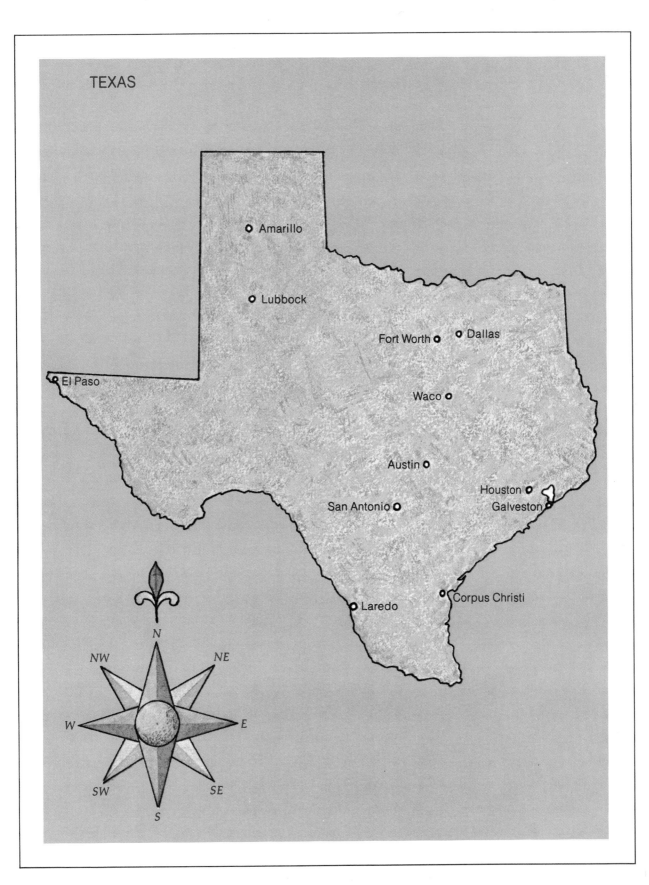

A TRANSPORTATION NETWORK

This is a place called Sometown. Copy the map, its title, the key, and the compass rose on a large sheet of paper. Then add a transportation network to the map. Follow the numbered instructions on page 273.

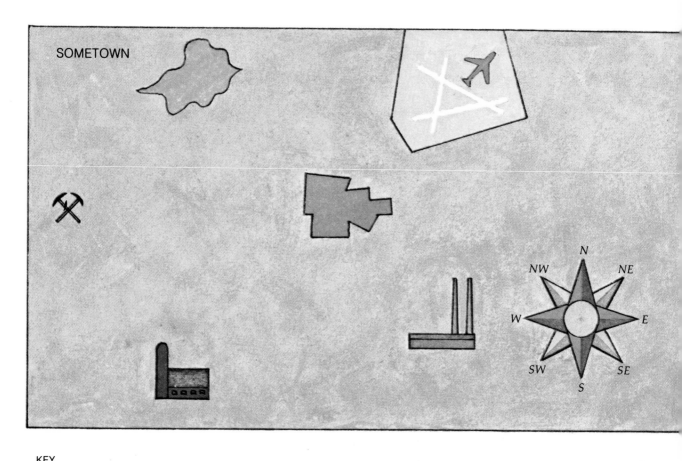

SOMETOWN

Follow the numbered instructions on page 273.

KEY

Town Center

Canning Factory

Farm

Lake

Airport

Coal Mine

Road

Railroad

Instructions

1. Look at the key to find the symbol for "road." Connect the airport and the center of Sometown with a road.

2. Connect the center of Sometown and the lake with a road.

3. Connect the farm and the center of Sometown with a road.

4. Connect the farm and the canning factory with a road.

5. Connect the canning factory and the center of Sometown with a road.

6. Look at the key to find the symbol for "railroad." Connect the coal mine and the center of Sometown with a railroad.

Answer these questions on another sheet of paper. Question 7 is done for you. *Each answer is a direction on the compass rose.*

7. Fruits and vegetables are sent from the farm to Sometown by moving *northeast*.

8. Coal is sent from the mine to Sometown center by moving _____ .

9. Workers from Sometown come to the factory by moving _____ .

10. People drive in to town from the airport by moving _____ .

11. People from Sometown go swimming and fishing at the lake by moving _____ .

(Check your answers with those on page 276.)　273

This is a photograph taken from an airplane. It is called an *aerial photograph.*

This map was made from the photograph.

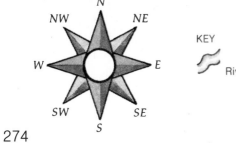

KEY

River

AERIAL PHOTOGRAPHS AND MAPS

On a separate sheet of paper, answer the following questions:

1. Here is a list of things. Some are in the photograph on the top of page 274. Some are not in the photograph. Write down those things in the list that you can find in the photograph.
   houses • streets • lake • river • hills • animals • cars • people • bank • school • church • hospital • football stadium • stores

2. The key to the map on page 274 has been left blank. Make a key to go with the map. Show at least five symbols. The first symbol has been done for you.

3. Below is another aerial photograph. Study it carefully. Then draw a map showing the things in the photograph. Make a key for the map.

Answers to Questions in
BUILDING MAP SKILLS

Finding the Way, page 266

1. west   2. north   3. school   4. stop sign   5. west

Estimating, page 267

1. Centerville   2. Cross Street is the shortest way.

Groups in a Small Community, pages 268–269

1. School Street   2. Lunt Street   3. north   4. four
5. Davis Street   6. west   7. Bill   8. Paul's

In-Between Directions, pages 270–271

1. southeast   2. southwest   3. northwest

A Transportation Network, pages 272–273

1–6. Ask your teacher to check your map.   7. northeast   8. east   9. southeast   10. southwest   11. northwest

Aerial Photographs and Maps, pages 274–275

1. Your list should include houses, streets, trees, church

2.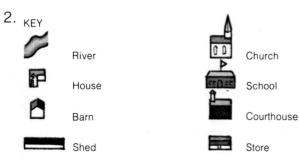

KEY

River

House

Barn

Shed

Church

School

Courthouse

Store

3. Ask your teacher to check your map.

ATLAS

THE UNITED STATES OF AMERICA

SOVIET UNION

Barrow

Kotzebue

Nome

Bering Sea

Fairbanks

ALASKA

CANADA

80°N

70°N

60°N

Bethel

Spenard • Anchorage

Gulf of Alaska

Juneau

Kodiak

Sitka

Ketchikan

50°N

Aleutian Islands

PACIFIC OCEAN

N

170°W 160°W 150°W 140°W 130°W

SCALE
0   200 Miles

0   200 Kilometers

ABBREVIATIONS

CONN.–CONNECTICUT
MASS.–MASSACHUSETTS
MD.–MARYLAND
N.H.–NEW HAMPSHIRE
N.J.–NEW JERSEY
R.I.–RHODE ISLAND
VT.–VERMONT
W. VA.–WEST VIRGINIA

KEY

National boundary

State boundary

⊙ National capital

○ State capital

• Other city

50°N

120°W 110°W 100°W 90°W 80°W 70°W

Vancouver

Seattle

Olympia

WASHINGTON

Portland

Salem

Eugene

OREGON

CANADA

Helena

MONTANA

NORTH DAKOTA

Bismarck

MINNESOTA

Lake Superior

Quebec

MAINE

Ottawa Montreal

Augusta

Montpelier N.H.

IDAHO

Boise

WYOMING

Pierre

SOUTH DAKOTA

WISCONSIN

St. Paul

Minneapolis

Lake Michigan

MICHIGAN

Lake Huron

Toronto

Lake Ontario

NEW YORK

VT.

Concord

Albany

Boston

MASS.

Providence

40°N

Sacramento

Carson City

San Francisco

San Jose

NEVADA

Salt Lake City

UTAH

Cheyenne

Denver

COLORADO

NEBRASKA

Madison

Milwaukee

Racine

Lansing

Detroit

Lake Erie

Buffalo

Hartford CONN. R.I.

New York

Omaha

Lincoln

IOWA

Des Moines

Chicago

ILLINOIS INDIANA

Springfield

Indianapolis

OHIO

Columbus

PENNSYLVANIA Trenton

Pittsburgh Harrisburg N.J.

Philadelphia

Baltimore DELAWARE

Dover

CALIFORNIA

Los Angeles

San Diego

PACIFIC OCEAN

Mexicali

ARIZONA

Phoenix

Santa Fe

NEW MEXICO

KANSAS

Topeka

Kansas City

Jefferson City

MISSOURI

St. Louis

Frankfort

W. VA.

Charleston

KENTUCKY

MD.

Annapolis

Washington, D.C.

Richmond

Norfolk

VIRGINIA

Raleigh

NORTH CAROLINA

ATLANTIC OCEAN

El Paso

OKLAHOMA

Oklahoma City

ARKANSAS

Little Rock

TENNESSEE

Nashville

Memphis

Birmingham

SOUTH CAROLINA

Columbia

Atlanta

30°N

Ft. Worth Dallas

TEXAS

Austin

Houston

San Antonio

LOUISIANA

Baton Rouge

New Orleans

MISSISSIPPI

Jackson

Montgomery

ALABAMA

GEORGIA

Tallahassee

Jacksonville

N

FLORIDA

Gulf of Mexico

Miami

Bahamas

MEXICO

Cuba

Hawaii inset

160°W 155°W

24°N

HAWAII

KAUAI

OAHU

Honolulu MOLOKAI

MAUI

22°N

PACIFIC OCEAN

HAWAII

Hilo

20°N

SCALE
0   200 Miles

0   200 Kilometers

SCALE
0   200   400 Miles

0   200   400   600 Kilometers

277

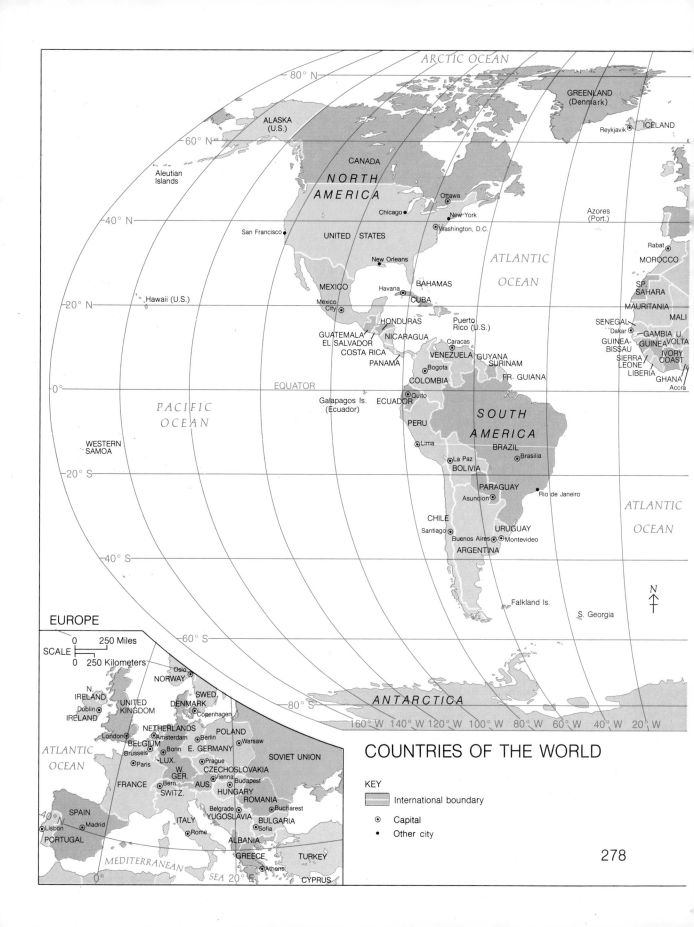

ARCTIC OCEAN

80° N

GREENLAND
(Denmark)

ALASKA
(U.S.)

Reykjavik ⊙ ICELAND

60° N

Aleutian
Islands

CANADA

NORTH
AMERICA

Ottawa ⊙
Chicago • New York

40° N

Azores
(Port.)

San Francisco •

UNITED STATES

⊙ Washington, D.C.

Rabat ⊙
MOROCCO

New Orleans •

Hawaii (U.S.)

MEXICO

Havana ⊙ BAHAMAS

20° N

SP.
SAHARA

MAURITANIA

Mexico
City ⊙

CUBA

MALI

SENEGAL ⊙
Dakar ⊙

GAMBIA U.
GUINEA VOLTA

HONDURAS

Puerto
Rico (U.S.)

GUINEA-
BISSAU

GUATEMALA
EL SALVADOR

NICARAGUA

Caracas •

SIERRA
LEONE

IVORY
COAST

COSTA RICA

VENEZUELA

GUYANA
SURINAM

LIBERIA

GHANA

PANAMA

⊙ Bogota

Accra

COLOMBIA

FR. GUIANA

EQUATOR

Galapagos Is.
(Ecuador)

ECUADOR

⊙ Quito

0°

PACIFIC
OCEAN

PERU

SOUTH
AMERICA

WESTERN
SAMOA

⊙ Lima

BRAZIL

La Paz •

Brasilia •

20° S

BOLIVIA

PARAGUAY

ATLANTIC

OCEAN

Rio de Janeiro •

Asuncion ⊙

CHILE

URUGUAY

Santiago ⊙

Buenos Aires ⊙ ⊙ Montevideo

ARGENTINA

N
↑

40° S

Falkland Is.

S. Georgia

60° S

ATLANTIC
OCEAN

OCEAN

ANTARCTICA

160° W 140° W 120° W 100° W 80° W 60° W 40° W 20° W

80° S

EUROPE

SCALE

0   250 Miles

0   250 Kilometers

Oslo ⊙
NORWAY

SWED.
DENMARK

COUNTRIES OF THE WORLD

N.
IRELAND

UNITED
KINGDOM

Copenhagen •

Dublin ⊙
IRELAND

NETHERLANDS

POLAND

Berlin •

Warsaw •

KEY

London ⊙
BELGIUM

Amsterdam ⊙

ATLANTIC

Brussels ⊙

Bonn ⊙

E. GERMANY

International boundary

OCEAN

⊙ Paris

LUX.

SOVIET UNION

⊙ Prague

W.
GER.

CZECHOSLOVAKIA

⊙ Capital

FRANCE

Bern ⊙

Vienna ⊙

Budapest •

• Other city

SWITZ.

AUS.

HUNGARY

ROMANIA

SPAIN

Belgrade ⊙

⊙ Bucharest

40° N

Madrid ⊙

ITALY

YUGOSLAVIA

BULGARIA

Lisbon ⊙

• Rome

Sofia ⊙

PORTUGAL

ALBANIA

278

MEDITERRANEAN

GREECE

TURKEY

SEA 20° E

⊙ Athens

CYPRUS

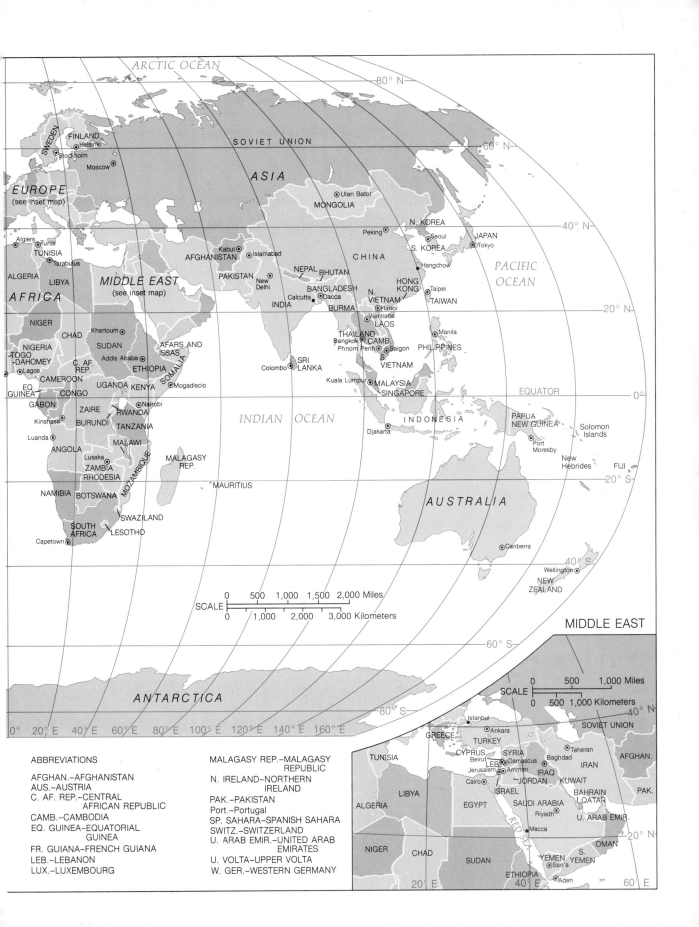

ARCTIC OCEAN

80° N

SWEDEN
FINLAND
Helsinki
Stockholm
Moscow

EUROPE
(see inset map)

SOVIET UNION

60° N

ASIA

Ulan Bator
MONGOLIA

40° N

N. KOREA
Peking
Seoul
JAPAN
S. KOREA
Tokyo

Algiers
Tunis
TUNISIA
Tarabulus

MIDDLE EAST
(see inset map)

Kabul
Islamabad
AFGHANISTAN

CHINA

Hangchow

PACIFIC
OCEAN

ALGERIA
LIBYA

PAKISTAN
New
Delhi

NEPAL
BHUTAN

HONG
KONG

Taipei
TAIWAN

AFRICA

INDIA

BANGLADESH
Calcutta
Dacca
BURMA

N.
VIETNAM
Hanoi

20° N

NIGER
CHAD

Khartoum

SUDAN

AFARS AND
ISSAS

Vientiane
LAOS

THAILAND
Bangkok
CAMB.

Manila

NIGERIA
TOGO
DAHOMEY
Lagos
C. AF.
REP.

Addis Ababa

ETHIOPIA

SOMALIA

Phnom Penh
Saigon
S.
VIETNAM

PHILIPPINES

CAMEROON
UGANDA
KENYA
Colombo
SRI
LANKA

Kuala Lumpur
MALAYSIA
SINGAPORE

EQ.
GUINEA
CONGO
Mogadiscio

EQUATOR
0°

GABON
ZAIRE
Nairobi
RWANDA
Kinshasa
BURUNDI
TANZANIA

INDIAN OCEAN

INDONESIA

PAPUA
NEW GUINEA

Solomon
Islands

Luanda
ANGOLA
MALAWI

Djakarta

Port
Moresby

Lusaka
MALAGASY
REP.

New
Hebrides
FIJI

ZAMBIA
RHODESIA
MOZAMBIQUE

20° S

NAMIBIA
BOTSWANA

MAURITIUS

AUSTRALIA

SWAZILAND

SOUTH
AFRICA
LESOTHO

Capetown

40° S

Canberra

Wellington

NEW
ZEALAND

SCALE
0   500   1,000   1,500   2,000 Miles
0   1,000   2,000   3,000 Kilometers

60° S

ANTARCTICA

80° S

MIDDLE EAST

0   500   1,000 Miles
SCALE
0   500   1,000 Kilometers

0°   20° E   40° E   60° E   80° E   100° E   120° E   140° E   160° E

40° N

Istanbul
Ankara
SOVIET UNION
AFGHAN.

GREECE
TURKEY
Teheran

ABBREVIATIONS

CYPRUS
SYRIA
Baghdad
IRAN

TUNISIA
Damascus

AFGHAN.-AFGHANISTAN
AUS.-AUSTRIA
C. AF. REP.-CENTRAL
    AFRICAN REPUBLIC
CAMB.-CAMBODIA
EQ. GUINEA-EQUATORIAL
    GUINEA
FR. GUIANA-FRENCH GUIANA
LEB.-LEBANON
LUX.-LUXEMBOURG

MALAGASY REP.-MALAGASY
    REPUBLIC
N. IRELAND-NORTHERN
    IRELAND
PAK.-PAKISTAN
Port.-Portugal
SP. SAHARA-SPANISH SAHARA
SWITZ.-SWITZERLAND
U. ARAB EMIR.-UNITED ARAB
    EMIRATES
U. VOLTA-UPPER VOLTA
W. GER.-WESTERN GERMANY

EB
Jerusalem
Amman
IRAQ
KUWAIT
PAK.

Cairo
JORDAN

LIBYA
ALGERIA
EGYPT
ISRAEL

SAUDI ARABIA
BAHRAIN
QATAR
U. ARAB EMIR.

Riyadh

Mecca

20° N

NIGER
CHAD
SUDAN
OMAN

YEMEN
S.
YEMEN
San'a

20° E
ETHIOPIA
40° E
Aden
60° E

GLOSSARY

In this glossary you will find important words and terms used in this book. Remember that many words have more than one meaning. The meanings given here are the ones that will help you most in reading this book. The number following each meaning tells you on what page you can find out more about the word or term.

aerial photographs pictures taken from the air (274).

astronomer a person who studies the stars and planets (69).

backbone the long bone that runs along the back of some animals. It helps to support the rest of the body. Humans have backbones. So have all other mammals (102).

belief something that a person thinks is true. Beliefs are an important part of human culture (133).

carbon dioxide a part of the air mixture (49).

community a network of groups that depend on each other and sometimes conflict and sometimes cooperate. People in a community share institutions, tools, and other parts of culture (161, 164).

compass rose a symbol on a map which shows where to find north, south, east, and west on the map (266).

conflict to act or speak against a person or group; to want to do things in a different way from others in a group (155).

cooperate to work or act with one or more persons for the same goal (154).

country a network of communities that depend on each other. These communities share some culture, and sometimes conflict and sometimes cooperate (176).

court place where a judge and other people listen to both sides of a conflict and try to decide fairly who is right (202).

culture the human way of living.

Tools, languages, institutions, and beliefs make up culture (121).

declaration   an official statement or announcement (203).

direction   the way in which anything goes, moves or points (266).

energy   the power that keeps things going (57).

estimating   giving a general idea of how big or how high something is without actually measuring it (267).

evaporate   to change from a liquid to a vapor or gas. When water goes from a river into the air to make a cloud, we say it *evaporates* (53).

explorers   people who travel to unknown places in order to discover new things (28).

family   a group that lives together and shares responsibility for the well-being of its members (191).

food chain   a chain of plants and animals where one link in the chain (one kind of plant or animal) is food for the next link in the chain (55).

global community   the largest group to which humans belong. All people and countries belong to this community (195, 198, 205).

goal   an aim, purpose, or place someone wants to reach (149).

goods   things made by humans that people want or need (176).

government   an institution that gives services and makes laws (rules) for a community (181).

group   two or more people who need each other, who speak or act together, and who do something or enjoy something together (146).

instinct   something a person or animal is born knowing. It makes the person or animal behave in a certain way (94).

institutions   things that people do over and over in the same way. Holidays are institutions. So are schools, banks, and libraries. Institutions are a part of culture (129).

interdependent   depending on or needing each other. Groups in a community may be interdependent. Countries in the global community are also interdependent (196).

interdependent networks networks which depend on each other. (See the meaning of network in this Glossary.) Countries which depend on each other for goods may form interdependent networks (196).

judge a person who listens to both sides and tries to decide fairly who is right. To judge is to weigh the choices and make a decision (202).

language a system of sounds, written words, or signals that make it possible for people to talk to each other or know what they mean. Language is a part of culture (126).

laws rules that are made by people or a government (181).

life-support system all the things that are needed to keep people alive (47).

locate find out where something is (269).

mammals the group of animals to which humans belong. Mammals have backbones and hair on their bodies. They are born alive from their mothers, and get milk from their mothers when they are babies. Mammals take care of their babies longer than any other kinds of animals (104).

microscope a tool used to make very small things look larger (85).

mixture what you get when different things are put together or combined (49).

network a system whose parts are connected to and depend on each other (162).

nonsocial animals animals that live alone (143).

oxygen a part of the air mixture. All living things need oxygen (49).

planet a body in space that moves around the sun (34).

recycled used over again instead of being thrown away (60).

rotate turn around in a circle; spin. Earth rotates. It takes 24 hours for Earth to make one full turn or *rotation*. This is what causes night and day (42).

satellite a body that travels around a planet, as the moon travels around

Earth. Human-made satellites are sent into space to get information about Earth or other planets (200).

scarce not enough; hard to come by or get (61).

services kinds of work others do for us or we do for others (180).

social animals animals that live together with other animals of the same kind. Humans are social animals (142).

soil the loose top layer of Earth in which plants can grow. Soil has water and minerals in it (55).

solar system the name for the sun together with all the planets that move around the sun (72).

space probe a spaceship that doesn't carry people but carries tools to gather information about space (76).

system something that is made up of parts that work together as a single whole (47).

transportation network a system of connecting routes over which people may travel or goods may be shipped (182, 272).

United Nations an organization (group) of people from many countries. The people meet to try to settle the problems they all have (203, 206).

UNICEF a group that works to help children all over the world. The letters of UNICEF stand for "United Nations Children's Emergency Fund" (198).

unique one of a kind. Each person is unique, because no one is exactly like anyone else (243).

voice print a chart of the sound waves made by a person's voice (254).

war one kind of force that is used to settle conflicts between countries or groups of people (207).

White House the building in Washington where the President of the United States lives and works (171).

CREDITS

The authors and publisher wish to express their appreciation to persons and organizations listed below for their courtesy in preparing illustrations and in making photographs available for reproduction. The following abbreviations have been used for a few sources from which many illustrations were obtained:
DPI — Design Photographers International; EPA — Editorial Photocolor Archives; NAS — National Audubon Society;
PR — Photo Researchers; Stock — Stock, Boston;
NASA — National Aeronautics and Space Administration;
GS — George Sheng; FS — Frank Siteman; EA — Erik Anderson;
GH — Grant Heilman

ILLUSTRATIONS

Angela Adams: 16–17, 59, 68, 84, 96–97, 112, 115, 116, 126, 127, 130, 220, 221, 235, 239, 240, 241

Marc Brown: 166, 167, 175, 176, 177, 178, 179, 205, 238, 255

James Curran: 46, 50, 53, 54, 56, 57, 61, 62, 161, 163

Jack Endewelt: 191, 192, 193, 194–195

Laszlo Gal: 32, 33, 36–37, 90–91, 105, 106, 120, 121, 125, 144, 145, 196, 197, 202

Rosekrans Hoffman: 98, 117, 138–139, 158, 174, 190, 208, 209, 230, 242, 256, 257, 261

Robert LoGrippo: 20–21, 22–23, 24, 25, 39, 41 (top), 71, 169, 170, 171, 172–173, 188, 200, 216–217

Raul Mina Mora: 27, 34, 41 (bottom), 42 (bottom left and right), 43, 72–73

Joel Snyder: 148, 149, 152, 156, 180, 181, 203, 204, 223, 224, 234

PHOTOGRAPHY

Cover Eric Simmons, Stock; (window) FS   2 Eric Simmons, Stock   3 FS 12 (top) FS; (bottom) NASA   13 (top left, top right, and bottom right) EA; (bottom left) Owen Franken, Stock 14–15 FS   18–19 Don Murie, Meyers Photo Art   26 K. E. Chellis, NAS   29 NASA   30–31 GS   35 Harvard College Observatory   40 EA, Stock; (bottom) James Pollock, NAS 42 Richard Balzer   44 (left) S. J. Krasemann, NAS; (top right) GH; (bottom right) John Burnley, NAS   45 (left) Rene Burri, Magnum; (right) EA   48 (top left) Owen Franken, Stock; (bottom left) NASA; (right) Shostal Associates   49 Marjorie Pickens   51 Ernest Braun   52 (top left) Helen Cruikshank, NAS; (top right) Wayne Miller, Magnum; (bottom left) S. J. Krasemann, NAS; (bottom right) C. G. Maxwell, NAS 58 GS   60 NASA   63 Elizabeth Wilcox   64 GS 65 GS   66 (top left) GS; (top right) Tony Florio, NAS; (bottom) FS   67 (left) GH; (right) Cal Harbert, NAS   69 (left) Historical Pictures Service-Chicago; (middle) Kitt Peak National Observatory; (right) NASA   70 (top) NASA; (bottom) GS 74 (top left, bottom left, and bottom right) The California Institute of Technology and The Carnegie Institution of Washington; (top right) NASA   76–77 Harvard College Observatory 80–81 Larry Nelson   82 (top left) GS; (middle left) Owen Franken, Stock; (bottom left) Harvey Lloyd from Peter Arnold; (bottom right) Yoram Kahana from Peter Arnold   83 (top left) Harvey Lloyd from Peter Arnold; (top right) GS; (middle right) Ellis Herwig, Stock; (bottom left) Diane Lowe; (bottom right) FS, Stock   85 (middle) GH; (left) K. W. Fink, Bruce Coleman, Inc.; (right) Hal Wagner   86 (top left) EA; (top right) GH; (bottom left and right) GH   87 GH   88 (top) GS; (bottom) GH 92 (top) NAS; (bottom left) GS; (bottom right) Rick Rizzotto 94 (top) GS; (bottom) GH   95 (top) Bruce Pitcher, NAS; (bottom left) GS; (bottom right) Rick Rizzotto   99 (top) Harry Engels, NAS; (bottom) GS   100 (top, middle left, bottom left and right) GS; (middle right) GH   101 all GS, except (top right) Warren Garst, Tom Stack Associates   103 all GS, except (bottom left) GH   104 GS   107 (top) GS; (bottom) Allan Power, NAS   108 (top) Hal Wagner; (bottom left) GS; (bottom right) GH   109 GS   110 (top and bottom) GH; (bottom) Bruce Coleman   111 (top left) GH; (bottom left and right) GS

118 (top) Bruce Coleman, Inc.; (bottom) H. Cruikshank, NAS 119 (top) FS; (bottom) GS   122 (top left) GH; (top right) Jacques Jangoux from Peter Arnold   123 (bottom left) Owen Franken, Stock; (bottom right) GS   124 (top left) EA, Stock; (middle) Owen Franken, Stock; (bottom left) John Running, Stock   128 (bottom left) Mark Bolton, NAS; (bottom right) EA 131 (top and bottom) GS   132 (top and bottom) GH 134 GS   135 GS   136 Jen and Des Bartlett from Bruce Coleman, Inc.   137 GS   140–141 Daniel Brody, Stock 142 (top left) Bruce Coleman, Inc.; (top right) Steve Wayman, PR; (bottom) GH   143 (top left) NAS; (top right) Steve Wayman, PR; (bottom) GH   146 Michal Heron   147 FS   150 (top) FS, Stock; (bottom) Michal Heron   151 FS   153 Mike Jaeggi, Meyers Photo Art   154 FS   155 GS   157 (top) Marion Bernstein; (middle left) William Rivelli, PR; (middle right) Daniel D. Sullivan; (bottom) FS, Stock   159 Peter Buckley, PR   160 (top left) EA; (top middle) FS; (top right) Raphal Macia, PR; (bottom left) Max Waldman, Magnum Photos; (bottom middle) FS; (bottom right) John H. Griffin   162 (top) Ken Heyman; (bottom left) F. B. Grunzweig, PR; (bottom right) T. A. Rothschild, Stock   164 (top left) Lizabeth Corlett, DPI; (bottom left) Daniel D. Sullivan; (bottom right) FS; (middle right) Tom Tracy, Meyers Photo Art   165 (top) FS; (bottom left) Taurus Photo; (bottom right) Owen Franken, Stock   176 (top) John Running, Stock   177 Mike Mazzaschi, Stock   178 (bottom) Burt Glinn, Magnum Photos   179 (top right) FS; (top left) Margaret McCarthy, Marcia Keegan   183 (top) FS; (bottom) FS, Stock   184 (top) Marjorie Pickens, Taurus Photo; (middle) Lizabeth Corlett, DPI   185 George Daniell, PR 187 (bottom) Davenport, Iowa, Chamber of Commerce 189 PR   198 Yoram Kahana, Taurus Photos   199 (top) Kay Muldoon, Meyers Photo Art; (bottom) ANI   201 (top) Irving Schild, DPI; (bottom) Irving Schild, DPI; (bottom) U.S. Coast Guard   206 ANI   207 CARE   210–211 Cary S. Wolinsky, Stock   212 (top) Russ Kinne, PR; (bottom right) Ken Heyman; (bottom left) FS   213 (top) Diane M. Lowe; (bottom right) Joan Kramer   214 Charles Harbutt, Magnum Photos   215 (left) Scott Ransom, Taurus Photos; (right) Don Murie, Meyers Photo Art   218 Rick Rizzotto   219 Ralph Breswitz, DPI 225 (bottom left) Cary Wolinsky, Stock; (bottom right) Harriet Arnold, DPI   227 FS   229 (left) George Roos, Taurus Photos; (right) Field Museum of Natural History 231 (bottom) GS   232 (top left) Susanne Anderson; (top right) Charles Anderson, Monkmeyer Press; (middle left) Jaeggi, Meyers Photo Art; (middle right) Michal Heron; (bottom left) Owen Franken, Stock; (bottom right) Michal Heron   233 (top) GS; (middle) Paul Conklin; (bottom) Lee Battiglia, PR 236 (top) FS; (bottom) F & H Schreider, PR   237 (top) Walter S. Clark; (bottom) Stanley Newfield, EPA   243 Clyde H. Smith from Peter Arnold   244 (top) George Halton, PR; (bottom) Carl Purcell, PR   245 (top) R. T. Peterson, PR; (bottom) FS, Stock   246–247 Joan Kramer   248 Ken Heyman 249 Rick Rizzotto   250 (left) Elliott Erwitt, Magnum Photos; (bottom) FS   251 Judith Aronson   252 FS   253 John Running, Stock   254 American Telephone and Telegraph 257 Roman Vishniac   258 NASA   259 EA   260 P. W. Grace, Taurus Photos   261 Frank I. Toman, Taurus Photos 262 FS   263 FS   264 Beebe, PR   265 Kathleen Arnold 274 Lowry Aerial Photo Service   275 Lowry Aerial Photo Service

MAPS AND CHARTS

34, 43 Raul Mina Mora   46, 50, 53, 56, 61 James Curran 72 Raul Mina Mora   161, 163 James Curran 166, 167 Marc Brown   171 Robert LoGrippo   175, 176, 177, 178, 179 Marc Brown   180, 181 Joel Snyder   182, 186, 187 David Lindroth   193, 194–195 Jack Endewelt 196, 197 Laszlo Gal   205 Marc Brown   234 Joel Snyder 238, 255 Marc Brown   266, 267, 268, 271, 272, 274, 276 Peter Cohen   277 Donnelley Cartographic Services 278–279 Robinson Projection, Donnelley Cartographic Services

INDEX

This index will help you find out about the people, places, and things in this book. The subjects are listed in the same order as the alphabet. Suppose you want to find where you can read about *groups.* First find the letter G. Then look down the column until you see the word. Under it are listed the different things about groups and where to find them in the book.